THREE PLAYS

The Gift, The Guest and
The Accounting

THREE PLAYS

The Gift, The Guest and
The Accounting

Frank E. Schacht

Rutledge Books, Inc. Danbury, CT

Rutledge Books, Inc.
107 Mill Plain Road, Danbury, CT 06811
1-800-278-8533
www.rutledgebooks.com

Manufactured in the United States of America

Cataloging in Publication Data
Schacht, Frank E.
   Three plays

   ISBN: 1-58244-041-7

   The gift -- The guest -- the accounting.

   1. Plays -- Collections.   2. Drama Collections.
812

Library of Congress Catalog Card Number: 99-66072

CONTENTS

⚔ The Gift ⚔

Summary

THE GIFT is an allegorical play based on themes well known and rekindled regularly toward the end of each year. The serious aspects of these themes such as the power of free will and the struggle between good and evil are presented in ways suitable for dramatic as well as entertaining effects.

Although there is a strong, deliberate contrast between the poverty of the cottage scenes and the splendor of Lucifer's throne, the basic requirements of scenery and costumes are simple. Thus, they will visually represent the basic meanings of the main themes and also hold down production costs.

Except for the dark sides in the character of Mike Balser, there is a general natural lightness that pervades speech and actions. In the Lucifer scenes, this lightness appears in the form of humor and irony. It is then carried to the very end of the play when the word 'gift' is defined in a particular way that offers a kind of linguistic dénouement for the story.

⚜ The Gift ⚜

Synopsis

THE GIFT presents in a simplified, modern version the timeless and ever popular themes of the Christmas season: a young mother and her carpenter husband, the birth of their first child, three visitors bringing gifts, helpful neighbors.

In contrast to these simple and well-known themes are the tricks and machinations of Lucifer and his two helpers who are trying their best to exploit the main characters and their intentions.

The play thus becomes a portrayal of the eternal struggle between good and evil. Further contrast, one of the basic requirements of good drama, is provided by the simplicity of the cottage scenes and the splendor of Lucifer's throne, the corresponding simplicity of the life of Joe and Mary Armes on the one hand and the actions of Lucifer and company on the other.

In summary, this is an excellent play, especially for the always exciting period at the end of the year. The simplicity of sets should hold down production costs. There is even room for possible musical background or accompaniment.

❧ Frank E. Schacht ❧

Persons, in order of appearance

Mary Armes: young housewife
Joe Armes: Mary's husband, factory worker
Malchen: their neighbor, a widow
Karl: landlord and factory owner: Karl Litus
Mike Balser: first visitor, former convict
Dolores Messenger: second visitor, a woman about 30 years old
Lucifer: head of the dark spirits
Samiel: Lucifer's helper
Uriel: Lucifer's aide
Henry: third visitor, about 17 years old, also known as 'the boy'

Places

Most of the play takes place in the main room of the Armes' cottage. The Lucifer scenes are played in front of lowered main curtain. During the last part of the final scene, stage is divided into front and rear part by a special, translucent curtain.

The time is the present.

A Play in Four Acts

⊀ ACT I, SCENE 1 ⊱

As curtain rises, we see the interior of a small simple cottage in the country: a room furnished with table, chairs, a rocker, sofa and other furniture as needed in the play. Backstage, there is a small kitchen annex. Two doors: A front door leading outside, the other to a back room. Mary Armes, very pregnant, is walking slowly from kitchen to table. For a short while she does various chores preparing a simple meal.

MARY: Each day it seems to be getting harder—the walking, the work, bending over—seems to be getting harder, each day. (Sits down in rocker, stiffly) And you, in there, you—inside. Wish you'd keep quiet for a few minutes. Just give me some rest, give me some sleep, will you. (Tries to get up) Keep quiet, or else come out. It's high time you did, anyhow. (Gets up, walks toward kitchen) Maybe this will make you behave, eh? Shake you up a little maybe. But—oh, my back. (Gesture) The pain in the back—the nerves—the strain. (Sits down again. Very tired, almost desperate, quiet) Why didn't you come out last month, you in there? Instead of giving me that false alarm?

Why didn't you come out, eh? Not ready yet, I guess. Or perhaps you like it better inside, eh? Don't blame you, really. Right now, it's getting too cold for anybody. (Gets up slowly, walks to stove backstage, checks pots, etc.) But—the pain was there last month. Just like I was told it would be. Just like they had said in the clinic, in the city, back in spring. (Pause) The pains—what did they call them? - Contractions— con—trac—tions—pains getting closer and closer. (Sits down again) But— you didn't want to come out last month, did you? (Puts hands over her stomach, sits for a few seconds, then gets up slowly and walks to door leading to back room. Knocks several times) Joe—Joe—you coming out? I fixed the breakfast for you. Oatmeal—

JOE: (From behind door to back room)Yeah—I'm coming, I'm coming. (Enters through back door) Seems to me I'm always coming—always coming into something new. Like all of us—coming, coming—new day, new job, new world—coming, coming, like the wind, like the snow—

MARY: (To herself) Wish more than ever, the baby was like you—coming—now—(To Joe) Better stop your words now, Joe. Hot air doesn't fit into the season, anyhow. (Sits down at table) And have something to eat before you're off to work. (Gets up, brings pot from stove to table. Joe sits at table)

I made oatmeal for you. Eat it while it's hot. And take a little milk too. There isn't too much of it left. (Pushes milk bottle toward Joe who empties contents on cereal bowl) And sorry, Joe, but we have no sugar left.

JOE: Thanks, Mary. How are you feeling today? Better?

MARY: I'm better when I sit down. Didn't sleep too much last night. The baby, you know—it's moving, moving around all the time. Keeps me awake, you know.

JOE: No sugar?

MARY: No—sorry, we're all out of it. But I'll get some, first thing, from your paycheck. I promise...

JOE: Oatmeal without sugar—like soup without salt— (Eats) I noticed we're short of wood, too. Must get some as soon as I come back this afternoon. Except that it gets dark too early now. Almost the end of the year, isn't it?

MARY: (Absentminded) But at least he didn't cry—

JOE: Cry?

MARY: The baby—didn't cry and keep you awake also. Not yet, anyhow. (Short laugh)

JOE: Don't think I'll be able to stand it.

MARY: What?

JOE: (Loud) First, the noise in the plant, all day long. Then I come home—and more noise. I—

MARY: Yes, I know. You told me. But—this noise will be different. Home noise—sort of natural, maybe

	even cute—
JOE:	Noise is noise, and none of it is cute. You don't know how bad it really is—in the plant, all day long—
MARY:	I know. You told me, many times (Gets up, brings pot from stove to table)
JOE:	(Louder still) I told you, but you don't understand. You don't _know_ because you aren't _there_. The big saws going up and down, up and down, all day long. (Demonstrates) With their hj-sh-ff—hj-sh-ff—sh—ff. (Makes saw noises, excited) And the big planer—rat-tat-tat-tat-tat—all day long—reminds me of a machine gun in those war movies we used to see in the city. Remember (Very loud) rat-tat-tat-tat-tat—It's enough to drive a person insane. (Pushes dish away from himself, gets up, walks up and down, very irritated)
MARY:	(Slowly and painfully) But at least—in your place—you have a little variety. All I have here—is these four walls.
JOE:	(Sarcastic) Variety—I have that, all right. Sometimes, the plant reminds me of one of those variety shows in the city. (Pause) I wish I had my own shop back—small as it was.
MARY:	Your own shop and your own debts—remember—on the machines, on the wood—
JOE:	But at least, it was mine, my own. You don't mind so much—anything, as long as it is your own.
MARY:	I hope you'll think this way about the baby, too.

JOE: (After a pause) Right now, I think I'll ask for a transfer to the paint shop. Not too much noise there, but then—there's the smell—

MARY: We'll have to get used to smells in this house, too. New smells, babies smell, you know.

JOE: (Irritated) The baby, the baby—can't you think or say anything else these days except baby—baby—

MARY: The baby is my life now, Joe. Our baby, it's our life.

JOE: Well, I'm going to work now I'm late as it is. (Gets up, gets his coat) Back to the saws, back to the noises. Wish I could stay home today.

MARY: (Gets up, goes to kitchen, puts lunch into paper bag) Here's your sandwich, your apples. Take care, and button up your coat. We might have snow this afternoon. (Puts lunch into lunch box)

JOE: (Walks around aimlessly for a while, then goes to Mary, kisses her) Take it easy, Mary. I'll try to be early tonight. See you. (Turns brusquely and walks out of front door without taking lunch box. Mary locks and bolts door behind him. Immediately, there are loud knocks on door. Mary opens up. Joe pushes door open but does not come in)

JOE: (Roughly) And lock the door behind me. Lock it and bolt it, and don't open it to strangers, you hear? The world is full of creeps these days—and out here, in the woods—and you in your condition. Take care, you hear? (Leaves quickly, pulls door shut behind him. Mary opens it and looks after him. Wind noises from outside. She closes door, locks and bolts it, as before)

MARY: Lock the door—lock it and bolt it. (Laughs) It's a joke. As if anybody ever came to see us out here. (Sits down, pause) The baby—of course, the baby will come to see us, maybe today. But he—she—whatever—has no choice. Must come, one way or another. (Laughs, gets up slowly) And people talk about freedom and all that— and the first thing any of us do in life, the first real action, and we have no choice. (Pause) Sorry, baby, sorry you have to come right here, in the woods practically. (Walks to window, dreamily. Wind outside increasing) Maybe Joe is right. We should have stayed in the city instead of moving out here, at least until after the baby was born (Cleans up table, does other chores) And you could have kept your own shop, Joe. It was yours, after all, with all the debts, and the waiting for orders that never came. It was more of life, Joe, it gave you dignity, self-respect, in spite of the debts, in spite of the failures—(Sits down) And you in there, you stop your kicking. Stop it. Just wait, you'll soon learn to listen to orders, too. You want to come out today? And start giving us orders. (Laugh, then sudden change in mood and speech) Hey—what will I do? Who'll help me? You, in there, if you

come today, at least wait until tonight when your
father gets home, okay? (Short pause, then
several persistent but soft knocks on front door.
Mary gets up, calls sharply) Yes—who is it?

VOICE: (From outside, mixed with half-suppressed
laughs) It's a neighbor of yours. I live a mile down
the road. May I come in? Could you open the
door? Please?

MARY: A neighbor? From down the road? Didn't even
know we had neighbors. And why is she laughing?
At me? Well—we'll see. I'll just have to open
up and see, I guess. So what— (She unlocks door
carefully. Enter Malchen, a middle-aged woman
in warm but poor and somewhat old-fashioned
clothes. She carries a shopping bag which she puts
on the table)

MALCHEN: Thank you, dear, thanks for letting me in. It's
windy outside. Getting colder, too.

MARY: Well—I don't know. I'm alone, sort of, that is
(Embarrassed) My husband is gone to work—

MALCHEN: I know. I saw him walk in the other direction. To
the furniture plant, right? (Muffled laugh)

MARY: (Has taken a tablecloth from a drawer. Malchen
takes her shopping bag off table, then helps Mary
with tablecloth) That's right. That's where he works.

MALCHEN: So—don't worry. And don't be afraid. We've
never met in person. My name is Elizabeth, but
everybody calls me Malchen (Laugh) as if I was

still a child.

MARY: You live down the road, you said? And why are you
laughing? —My name is Mary, by the way, Mary
Armes. My husband is Joe, Joe Armes. (Malchen
extends her hand which Mary shakes timidly)

MALCHEN: Nice to meet you in person at last, Mary. I don't
really know why I'm laughing. Perhaps I'm getting
old, or perhaps because you lock your door
so carefully. (Confused laugh) And I do live down
the road, in a cottage like yours. And my
husband used to work in the furniture plant, just
like yours does now. And I pay my taxes and get
my wood, regularly—

MARY: (Disregards last words, sits down, embarrassed) If
you'll excuse me, but I don't feel too good right
now, especially when I'm on my feet. (Pause then
sudden loud knock on front door)

JOE: (From outside) Open up, Mary. For God's sake,
open up, quick.

MARY: (Gets up slowly, walks to front door) Okay,
okay. I'm coming, coming. (Unlocks door, Joe
bursts inside)

JOE: What took you so long, in all damnation?
Where's my lunch box? Why didn't you give it to
me before? Why did I have to forget it? Always
the forgetting, always the dumb ox —that's me.

MARY: Okay, okay. Quiet down already, will you? Here it
is. Here's your lunch, right here. — We have a

visitor, Joe. One of our neighbors—

JOE: I'm late as it is. Boss is going to kill me—Damn forgetfulness of mine— (Storms out front door) See you later, Mary. Take care. (Mary locks door behind him. Deep sigh)

MALCHEN: (Laughs) You always lock your door so carefully? There's no need to, out here, you know. (She gets busy doing various chores. Mary sits down)

MARY: Got so used to locking doors when we lived in the city. Bad habit, I guess. And you?

MALCHEN: Me? Oh no, I never lock my doors anymore. I've lived around here for many years now— besides there's not much worth stealing in my place. And the car is in the garage, anyhow— (Unpacks her shopping bag) Here—I brought you a bottle of milk, just in case. You must excuse me (Laughs) but I've been watching you a little, ever since you moved in. You must be getting pretty close now, huh?

MARY: That's kind of you to bring us milk. Yes, I'm getting pretty close now. (Reaches for bottle) Funny—a bottle of milk. First present since we moved in here. Except of course for Joe's job. It doesn't pay much, but at least it's steady. —You said your husband used to work in the plant? Did he make furniture, too?

MALCHEN: That's right. It was years ago. We saw this ad in the paper offering a job and a place to live, in

the country. So we took it, we moved... (Busy
with chores)

MARY: (Gets up to help her) You too? Same as happened
to us. Just imagine. We were down in the dumps.
I mean—really down. There wasn't much work in
the city. All we had was debts, it seemed. Over our
heads. And the baby...Then we saw this ad. We
came out here for an interview with the foreman.
We sold everything we had, paid off the debts and
came out here to start all over. —God, baby, be
quiet, and don't start hurting again, you hear?

MALCHEN: Hurtin'? You hurtin'?

MARY: Yes—I guess so—same as a couple of weeks ago.
But that time it went away again. So—never mind.
(Sits down) There, this is better.

MALCHEN: And how does your husband like the work?

MARY: The work is okay. It's in his line, he's a carpenter.
But he doesn't like the noise of the machines, the
big saws especially. Drives him crazy, he says.
(She mimics Joe's earlier noises and description)

MALCHEN: The noise, the machines—I know.

MARY: But at least it's steady work..

MALCHEN: As long as it lasts...

MARY: What do you mean...as long as...I thought it was
permanent. The foreman said so in the interview.

MALCHEN: Nothing is permanent, dear. (Gets ready to
leave) But never mind. I talk too much.

MARY: Thanks again for the milk and for all the work you

did...a real help for me, today especially. Don't go yet. Do you have to? Let me turn the radio on. (Does so. Bits of music, ads, a carol)

MALCHEN: Yes, I must go. If you need more help, just call, you hear? (Laughs)

MARY: Call? Where? How?

MALCHEN: Call—shout—scream, whatever. I won't be far, just down the road. Take care. Good-bye. (Leaves by main door which Mary locks carefully)

MARY: Strange person. Well, the world is full of them, and new ones are born every minute. Brought a present, too. Runs her own welcome wagon, I guess. Like in the city. Let's see it again; what did she bring us? (Sits down in rocker with shopping bag on her lap. Takes out milk bottle) How nice of her. Our first present—and it's for the baby. You hear that, you, inside? It's for you. But that doesn't mean you should start kicking again, does it? You must be a boy—can't wait until you're old enough to play football. (Puts milk bottle back into shopping bag) Hey—wait. There's something else. Another bottle (Pulls out a pint of liquor) What does it say on it? Vodka? Hm—haven't seen one of these for along time. Grandma Domski used to have them in her house, bless her soul. On her cupboard. Used to take a little nip every so often. 'Fodka,' she used to say in her funny accent. 'Fodka—is just water, child. Is good for you, a little.

14

Da.' (She looks at bottle again, turns it around, reads) There's a note glued to the back. Let's see: 'For you, dear neighbor. You might need a little of it one of these days. I like to take a little myself on cold days. Have a drop. It's good for you. Malchen.' So—two presents in one day. Two bottles. (Gets up) I'll put the milk outside the window (Does so) and then have a taste of this— water. Hm—not bad. Have another. (Mimics) Is good—da. (Turns radio up) Grandma Domski, bless her soul. Raised me from a child. (Sits down in rocker) Had many friends—had heart too— miles of it, as it says, somewhere. (She dozes off, bottle in her lap. Radio plays 'What Child is This?' (Mary hums along for a short while as lights dim. Curtain. Short pause)

❧ ACT I, SCENE 2 ❧

As curtain rises, lights come back on but are dimmer than in Scene 1. Radio plays softly as before. Mary has fallen asleep in rocker. A few seconds of this peaceful scene, then suddenly loud noises from outside door. Heavy items are thrown on front porch. Loud knocks on front door)

MARY: (Wakes up, shakes, drop bottle on floor) Joe— where are you—Joe—

VOICE FROM OUTSIDE: Anybody home? Open up. Open up.

MARY: (Gets up slowly. Confused. Holds her head, stomach) Okay. Okay. Coming, coming. (Walks aimlessly around room) What's the matter with everybody today? For weeks—nobody. Nobody except us. And today—everybody. Everybody drops in. Or just drops—something. (Pause) And that knocking. Knocking outside, knocking inside. (Puts hand on stomach) Okay, okay. I'm coming. Who is it, anyhow? (Unlocks door carefully) Who is it? (Enter Karl Litus. Middle-aged, arms full of wood, dressed for winter. Pushes door open, slowly)

KARL: It's me, just me, delivering the wood. Pardon the racket I made, lady. But I've got rounds to make before its gets dark, delivering wood, as usual—

MARY: As usual?

KARL: Sure. It goes with your home, the wood. Didn't you know? Didn't they tell you?

MARY: (Retreats toward kitchen. Karl follows her to stove, dumps wood there) No, they didn't. (Timid)

KARL: Of course—it's your first winter here, right? (He brings in more wood. Mary tries to help him)

MARY: (Stumbles) Oh—

KARL: No—don't pick it up. I'll do that for you. Here— you want it stacked back here?

MARY: Yes. Thanks. (Sits down) Okay—that's better.

KARL: Let me fill up the stove for you, too. It's getting colder outside, Your husband should be back soon, right?

MARY: (Uncertain, timid) No—not until evening. He works in the furniture plant, down the road a way. You know the place?

KARL: (Slow, deliberate) I know the place. I know it well, very well—You have enough wood for a while— Anything else I can do for you?

MARY: No, nothing, thanks—yes, there is. Could you turn the radio up a little. It's getting harder and harder for me to move now, and I think— (Karl turns radio up, goes toward backstage. Sudden loud steps outside front door. Loud knocks)

JOE: Open up, Mary. It's me, Joe. Open up. It's cold outside.

MARY: Come right in, Joe. The door's not locked. (Door is pushed open. Wind and snow. Joe enters)

JOE: I told you to keep the door locked all the time. We always do. (Walks briskly to her chair) You must listen to me—

MARY: Joe—you listen to me—I think the baby's coming (She leans back in rocker, clutches her stomach)

JOE: (Takes off his coat, looks around the room, does not notice Karl) Foreman came around right after lunch. Told us to go home early today, take the rest of the day off, with pay. Christmas Eve.

MARY: (Again tries to get up) Joe—the baby—

JOE: So—I'm home early for a change. What do you know. Christmas. Forgot all about it was so close. Just plain forgot. That's just like me—(Busy) On the other hand, not my fault, really. Always does it to us—Christmas. Sneaks up like the first snow in winter, then comes up big and knocks out your week, your days, your routine—Well, so what— I'm home early today. No more noises today or tomorrow. Okay with me—Tell you what, Mary, let's make a big fire. I see you got more wood. (At stove) Hey—where did all the new wood come from?

KARL: (Steps forward) I brought it in.

JOE: You brought it in? And who are you? (To Mary) Is that why you don't lock the door? So that strangers can just walk in?

MARY: (Angrily) Oh, don't be a fool, Joe. He just brought
        us some wood. Said it goes with the house.
        Malchen said so too. (Groans) Besides, Joe—

JOE: And everybody at work got mad at the boss, how
        inconsiderate he was, they said, not letting us
        know ahead of time we'd have half a day today.
        Maybe he thought nobody would show up for
        work if he told us in advance. Called him all sorts
        of names. Me too—just felt like doing it. It was like
        some sort of celebration—funny. (Laughs)

KARL: Maybe he wanted it to be a surprise, a good
        surprise, Christmas bonus, sort of—It happened
        before in the plant, but you wouldn't know,
        of course.

JOE: (More and more excited) Yes sir, called him all
        sorts of names, we did. Some crazy party— But
        now, I'm glad I came home, so I can see for myself
        what's going on. (To Karl) You're right, mister—
        some surprise—

MARY: (Screams at him) Joe—help me, I need help.
        (Gets up)

KARL: (Quiet and firm) Don't be silly, Joe. And listen
        to me—

JOE: (Shouts) No, you listen to me, mister! You finished
        your work here, right? You brought the wood?
        Now—get out of here. Get out (Hustles Karl to
        front door, opens it, pushes him outside. Snow,
        wind, noises)

KARL: (Turning to Joe) Your wife—take care of her. The baby's coming. (Comes back inside)

MARY: (Strangely quiet) Joe—please—get that bucket and put it under my chair, will you? The pain is strong now. The baby is coming—

JOE: What? What did you say? The baby? Oh yes, I forget—

MARY: Get me my coat, too, Joe. There's a woman who lives down the road about a mile, she says. Name is Elizabeth—no, Malchen. You met her, Joe. (She screams again, but Joe stands absolutely quiet. Mary moves toward door, takes her coat. Confusion, the door is pushed open, enter Malchen)

MALCHEN: Back I am, with the wind, with the snow. (Laughs) Been waiting to hear from you, been waiting outside, in the car. Come along, dear. The car is nice and warm. We'll take you to town, to the hospital. Come along.

MARY: No, don't take me. Don't take me away. (Screams) Let me lie down, right here, please. (Screams)

MALCHEN: (To Joe) You take care of the fire in the stove. Make sure you keep this place warm. And make plenty of hot water, just in case. (To Karl) You, mister (Laugh)—help me with this young woman. Help me take her to the car. (Both put coat on Mary, lead her to front door)

JOE: (Suddenly alert, stops working at stove) Let me

help, too. Your scarf, Mary. Take your scarf.
(Rushes after Malchen and Karl)

MALCHEN: She'll be all right, young man. (Laughs) You just
tend to the fire for a while. I'll come back and get
you later on. First, let's get Mary to the hospital.
(Pulls bottle from her coat pocket, gives it to
Mary) Here, Mary, have a little, from my bottle. Is
vodka, is just water, is good. (Laugh) (Mary takes
bottle, drinks, spits, screams. Malchen takes bottle
from her, takes long drink herself. Laughs. She,
Karl and Mary exit front door. Joe closes it, locks
it. He wanders around aimlessly for a while,
works at stove, fire. Wind noises very strong,
cloud of smoke from stove. Confusion. Joe
unlocks front door. Curtain)

❧ Act II, Scene 1 ❧

The same day, several hours later, early afternoon. Lights dim on stage, artificial fire in stove. Joe sits in rocker, asleep. Wind noises, radio, weather report of winter storm. This scene for a short while after curtain has gone up. Front door is pushed open slowly. Enter visitor I, Mike Balser. He is bundled up but poorly dressed, carries a travel bag over his shoulder. Age about 30 to 35. Steps carefully, looks around.

MIKE: Is this the right place? I wonder. It says in the letter (Pulls letter from inside pocket) 35 Cottage Row. (Checks number on outside of front door, reads) 'Go to 35 Cottage Row, Loweville, deliver the package and receive your free gift. It will make you a wealthy man.' (Laughs, brushes snow off coat, unbuttons it) A weather man. After a life of tough luck, and where I'm coming from —a wealthy man. It's a laugh—almost. (Louder) Well, where is it? Where is it?

JOE: (Wakes up. Confused) Huh? Where is it? Where is what? The baby? Mary? I—I don't know—

MIKE: Well, well. (Rubs his hands, steps to stove) There's somebody, after all. (Roughly) Hey, you—get up and come over here.

JOE: (Still confused. Gets up, walks to Mike, cautiously)
And who are _you_? The doctor? Is the baby okay?
Anything wrong? Are you—the police?

MIKE: The doctor? This is getting better and better.
About time, too. (Walks around looking at every
thing) Except—don't mention the police, okay?
(Sits down) No, a doctor I am not. For once in my
life, I'm just—obeying orders, following
instructions. Like it says in this letter. (Holds letter
up) And—here's your present— (Pulls package
from coat pocket, but doesn't give it to Joe) You
can have it, but first, give me my gift. Or show me
at least where it is. I don't want to stay longer in
this place than I have to—-

JOE: Gift? What gift? What are you talking about? I
don't understand. And who are you, anyhow?

MIKE: (Gets up, advances toward Joe) Now listen here,
Mac—

JOE: The name's Joe, Joe Armes—

MIKE: Okay—Joe—Joe Armes—don't you try playing
games with me, you hear—(Grabs Joe's shirt,
shakes him) Now—where is it? (Noise of car
outside. Car doors slammed. Quick steps to front
door. Door is flung open. Enter Malchen,
laughing. Snow, wind)

MALCHEN: I knew it—-have known it since the summer—
when that baby arrives at 35 Cottage Row, I'll be

there too. (Laughs) I knew it all the time—

JOE: (Wrenches free from Mike, pushes him back. Urgently to Malchen) The baby? Where is it? And where's Mary? Are they okay?

MALCHEN: (Hustling about) I see you kept the place warm. Good. And you moved the sofa close to the stove. Good. It's going to be cold tonight. Very cold—

JOE: The baby—for God's sake—the baby, and Mary— tell me—

MALCHEN: And help me with this kettle, will you? Get it over to the other side of the stove—there. (Joe obeys) And you (To Mike) take this bucket and get more water for me. Please. The pump is behind the house. Hope it isn't already frozen up. We'll need plenty of water— (Mike puts letter and package back into coat pocket, shakes his head, cusses, stares at Joe and Malchen but obeys and exits front door) Yes—all is okay in here. I think I'll go and get them.

JOE: (Blocks her way) My wife, lady—how is she? And the baby?

MALCHEN: Please—Joe—put some more wood on the fire, will you? (Joe obeys) You're a father now, by the way. Congratulations. Your wife had a boy, beautiful and healthy. Both are waiting outside, in the car, both warm and fairly comfortable. (Pause) Sorry—we didn't make it to the hospital. Just to my house. The garage. That's where he was born—quick, no complications. Cute boy—strong woman, too, your Mary. Very tired, and very happy, right now. But—go and get them yourself. All is ready inside. Go and bring them in. (Joe, suddenly alert, drops wood, rushes outside) I knew it—all those long years, I knew it. There was some reason why I got stuck in this place on Cottage Row. (Busy) Wasn't so bad before my husband passed away—he always said: 'Just be patient, there's a reason, just wait... 'Well, for years I waited and waited, and now I've seen— (Pause) For years, not a soul—and now—first the young couple last summer—then—the baby—I knew it— (Door is pushed open, enter Mary, holding baby (doll). She walks slowly, is supported by Joe and Karl)

JOE: I moved the sofa near the stove. Easy now, Mary— come over here and lie down. Give me the baby, I'll hold it for you—

MARY: Him—Joe—it's a boy. So—you hold _him_ (Hands baby to Joe) And get me the milk that Malchen brought us. We'll heat it up. (Stretches out on sofa) My God—this feels good. I never thought that birth might be like this—out here—nowhere—in a garage—so much pain and so much happiness. Oh Joe, I'm so happy now. Give the baby back to me, our baby, our boy. (Joe hands baby to her. Pause. Door is pushed open and Mike returns with bucket)

MIKE: Here it is—here's your water. Took me an eternity to chop the ice off the pump. Now—where is this—this gift you promised me?

MARY: (Weakly) Who's this, Joe? Tell him not to make so much noise. He'll wake the baby.

JOE: I don't know who he is. (To Mike) Mister—what's you name? And what do you want?

MIKE: The name's Mike—Mike Balser. Not that it matters—and here's the present I was told to deliver—(Gives package to Mary who begins to unwrap it) Now—give me _my_ present, _my_ gift— and I'll be going.

JOE: Gift? I have no gift for you. I told you already. But— thanks for bringing in the water. Could you help me pour some in this pot, and put it on the stove?

MIKE: Do it yourself. I've done enough.

MALCHEN: Here—let me help you—easy now—(Both busy with water, pot, etc., while Mike goes into a corner)

MIKE: (To himself first, then to all) No gift? What do they mean—no gift? It says so, in the letter—You mean all these months, all these nights in my cell—I've been dreaming about a gift. (Louder) The gift promised in is letter. (Shows letter) And here I'm getting out just before Christmas, I spend my last penny on a bus ticket to get out here—and now—no gift? (Last words very loud)

MALCHEN: (From kitchen) Sh-sh, mister, not so loud—
the baby—

MIKE: The baby—never mind, the baby. (Threatening) I
don't know about you people, and about this place.
But—where I've been these last few years—you
don't pull this kind of deal and get away with it.
Not after you put in writing. (Reads letter) So—I'll
tell you what— (Pulls long knife from his coat, tests
edge with his thumb) You think about his, think
very hard. Either you give me what I came for, or I
take what I can get. (Walks to sofa, sits on chair near
it) You think very hard, Joe, you understand?

MARY: (Has finished unwrapping Mike's package) Look,
Joe, everybody, look—it's—another bottle—

MALCHEN: (Laughs, take bottle) Let me see what it says.
(Reads, pronounces carefully) Par-e-gor-ic—dilute
if necessary before use for children or adults.
(Reads again, shakes head, laughs)

MIKE: (Roughly) Give it back—I didn't bring it here to
have you make fun of it. (Takes bottle, opens it,
sniffs, takes a swallow, spits) God—no—not this
kind of stuff. Bitter like any damn drug. Bitter—
not that again, had enough of that—What's it
good for, anyhow?

MALCHEN: Diarrhea.

MIKE: Shit. (Pause) Well—you heard what I said. You
give, or else—I take. You got five.

MALCHEN: (Cautiously) Five?

MIKE: Five minutes, lady—

JOE AND MARY: To do what?

MIKE: To get me whatever it is that's promised in the
          letter. (Waves letter and knife) Or else.

JOE: (Slowly) I told you already. I don't know anything
          about the letter, about any gift—<u>We</u> didn't
          promise you anything.

MARY: (Weakly) Would you mind if the baby and I went
          into the bedroom? I feel cold suddenly, cold and
          weak. (Joe and Karl get ready to take Mary
          to bedroom)

MIKE: Sit down, all of you. You got three left—

MALCHEN: (Walks up to Mike) Now why would you be so
          stubborn, mister?

MIKE: Stubborn? (Loud)

MALCHEN: (Louder) And unreasonable.

MIKE: (More and more intense) Unreasonable? For ten
          years I've been sitting and waiting—ten years for
          killing a woman in anger. A prostitute, she was,
          you might as well know. For years I paid for a life
          wasted on stealing, drugs, killing. I earned time
          for good behavior—you know how hard this is?
          Good behavior? In prison? Well—I earned my
          time, and here comes this letter just before I'm due
          for parole—first letter I ever get in prison—I open
          it, read it. Somebody promises me a gift—free—if
          I follow instructions. Okay, I follow them. I get

special permission from the P.O. I spend my last
nickel for a bus ticket and get here—and now you
say you never wrote the letter, nor promised me a
gift. And you call me unreasonable, stubborn—
you got one—one minute. (Leans back in his chair
exhausted, very tense. All have been listening
intently. Soft baby noises from sofa)

MALCHEN: (Softly) You are right, mister. And I apologize.
Tell you what—here—have a drink from my
bottle. (Pulls bottle from coat) And let the men
take Mary and the baby to the bedroom.

MIKE: (Takes bottle, opens it, sniffs, takes long drink
while Joe and Karl take Mary and baby to
bedroom. Karl returns alone, takes piece of fire
wood and walks behind Mike's chair where he
stands and waits. Lights dim and out. Brief pause)

⚔ Act II, Scene 2 ⚖

Scene unchanged, lights a little dimmer than in Scene 1. Joe returns from bedroom.

JOE: She fell asleep and the baby too. We'd better keep the milk warm. They'll want some when they wake up.

MALCHEN: (Checks milk on stove, etc.) Sleep—that's good. It means they're healthy, both of them. Sleep can cure anything. 'More sleep, less trouble,' as my husband used to say. (Knock on front door. Enter visitor II, Dolores Messenger, a woman around 30, stylish dress, boots, fur coat. Clutches a handbag)

DOLORES: Good evening. (Looks around for a short while and everybody looks at her. Both Mike and Joe get up, Mike sits down again)

JOE: (Embarrassed, hesitating) Good evening—sit down, please. We have no bed—but we have room to sit. (Closes door, locks it) Who are you?

DOLORES: Dolores—Dolores Messenger (Sits down) My friends always call me 'Messy', for short—did it from way back in school. My family, too, except for my mother. She preferred 'Missy' (Unbuttons fur coat—good dress, good figure) If you lived in the city, you might have heard about me— (Looks at Joe, carefully)

JOE: We don't live in the city any more. Used to, but no longer—moved here last summer.

DOLORES: (Looks carefully at Mike who has sunk back in his chair) I'd say you don't live in the city. (Looks around room) It took the cab all afternoon to get here. The driver said he could only take me to the beginning of Cottage Row because he might get stuck in the side street. Don't really blame him, with all this snow, suddenly. Except that the ride cost me a fortune. (Takes her coat off, lays it carefully over back of chair, looks around) I see you're having a little party here. Christmas Eve, of course. Got something to drink, too? Maybe?

MALCHEN: I'll make you some tea. I have the water on the stove already. It'll take just a second. (Pours tea, brings cup to Dolores)

DOLORES: Thanks, lady. This is good. Thanks very much. Now—to our business.

JOE: Business?

DOLORES: (Loud) Your letter. (Mike stirs in his chair)

JOE: What letter?

DOLORES: (Pulls letter from pocketbook) This letter— (Holds it up for all to see)

Joe: (Painfully) Oh no, not again—not another letter, not another promise. Oh no—(Mikes sits up in his

chair, holds his letter and knife in his hands,
watches carefully)

DOLORES: (Nonchalantly, but still loud) I thought _you_
might not know anything about it. _You_ couldn't
possibly have sent me all that money.

MIKE: Money? (Half rises from chair. Karl still behind
him now moves a little closer, but Mike does not
see him)

DOLORES: (Sharply, to Mike) And who are you, may I ask?

MIKE: Balser—Mike Balser. (Gets up) I got a letter too,
like you—but no money—

DOLORES: Let me see it.

MIKE: (Looks at her, does not give her his letter) You—
come from the—big house too? Upriver? You
don't—quite look that way—

MALCHEN: Have some more tea. You too, Joe—have some.
It'll warm you insides—good for you
(Pours several cups)

DOLORES: Big house—yes, in a way, I do. (Laughs) It's a big
house, but not _that_ big house, Mike, and I'll tell
you. (Mike sits down, Karl steps back) It was a
couple of days ago that I got this letter. Registered
mail—imaging. Money in it—500 dollars. Cash.
Instructions with it, too—(Reads) 'With the
enclosed money buy yourself a new coat, new
dress, boots, then take a cab to the following
address: 35 Cottage Row in Loweville. Hand over
the enclosed envelope and receive your free gift.'

MIKE: (Moves his chair closer to Dolores. Karl moves behind him) Free gift—just like my letter. (Laughs loud)

DOLORES: What's so funny?

MIKE: Funny—funny? (He laughs loud for a while. Dolores joins in, so does Malchen. Everybody seems relaxed, except Karl who stands in his place behind Mike's chair, silently) I got the same kind of letter—except for the money of course. And I had a package to deliver, too, and guess what was in it—

DOLORES: Let me see—what was in it? In your pack age? A gold watch, on a chain—

MIKE: A gold watch—that's really funny now. Guess again. I'll give you a hint—a bottle—

DOLORES: Of gin—

MIKE: Of paregoric—you know the medicine, sort of drug, they use it for diarrhea— (Laughs loud and all join in once more) And now—these two people, Joe here and his wife Mary—they—they don't know anything about the whole thing. And they haven't got any gift. Get it? No gift. (Pause, then loud laughter from Malchen. Joe shakes his head, finally laughs too. Karl remains where he is, does not laugh) Here—here is my letter. And let me see yours. (All laugh for a while in a more and more forced, unnatural way. Mike and Dolores exchange letters. Sudden silence as they both read.

Baby cries suddenly from bedroom)

MALCHEN: Not so loud—see what you did? Woke the baby.

DOLORES: Baby? Where's the baby? (Gets up and walks to bedroom door. Listens. Baby cries) Sounds brand new. (Pause) There's a gift, Mike, a brand-new baby. It's some gift, for somebody. (Loud laughter again, then abrupt silence as bedroom door opens and Mary appears holding baby. Spotlight on them for a few seconds)

MARY: The baby is hungry. Can I have the bottle now?

DOLORES: (Steps toward Mary) Well, I'll be damned. So— there _is_ a baby. I didn't just dream about it. God— what a party. What's going on here? (Holds her head, goes back to her chair, sits down. Mary and baby sit down in rocker. Malchen hands Mary the bottle. Mike gets up, leaves knife and letter in his chair, walks over to Dolores. Karl quickly takes knife from Mike's chair)

MIKE: (To Dolores, loud and distinct) And what did you do with the money? Five hundred dollars, you said?

DOLORES: (Peeved) Can't you see what I did? I spent most of it on new clothes. Did as I was told. Can't you see? What's the matter with you, anyhow?

MIKE: (Follows Dolores around) I've been locked up for too long, that's what is wrong. I guess—(Looks at her) Yeah—I can see—okay. I can see now. And I like what I see.

DOLORES: (Goes back to her chair. Sits down) That's better.

But tell me—why the knife? You—some kind of
butcher? Or maybe you want to carve the turkey,
hun? (Loud laugh)

MIKE: The knife. (Jumps back toward his chair) Where is
it? Where is my knife, goddammit -

DOLORES: (Walks over to Mike's chair) Forget the knife.
(Puts hand on shoulder) Can't you see—you
won't need one around here. Not for a while,
anyhow. (Mike pushes her hand away, violently,
then gives her a long look which she returns without flinching. A few seconds of this contest)

MIKE: Okay—if you say so. (Shrugs and sits down) No
knife, then. No gift, no nothing. (Slumps back in
his chair)

DOLORES: (Sits down, smoothes her dress) If I had known,
if I had only known—

MIKE: What—

DOLORES:What kind of place this was, this 35 Cottage
Row—and what kind of people—-

MIKE: So—you wouldn't come, maybe?

DOLORES: I wouldn't have bought this new fur coat—
rabbit—yech—I would have worn my winter coat
instead. And no new dress—have plenty of old
ones. Perhaps new boots—yes, new boots.

MIKE: And?

DOLORES: And—I would have brought the money here,
with me, as a gift—

MIKE: Too bad you didn't. But orders are orders, I guess.

Besides—you look nice in new clothes.

DOLORES: Thanks, Mike. One of the few sincere compliments I've had for sometime. Thanks. (They exchange looks) Besides—I still have the other envelope. The one I'm supposed to hand over (Pulls it from her pocketbook, hands it to Mary) Here, young mother, for you.

MARY: Another present? For me? For us? It can't be. I'm getting all confused—don't' know what to open first. (Pause. Mary reaches for envelope, but before she can take it, Mike has jumped up and snatched envelope from Dolores' hand)

MIKE: Here—I'll take that. Must have money in it, I bet. (Loud, while getting up) At least I get something out of all this funny business. (Waves envelope, grabs his coat, runs toward front door) See you, everybody. Take care, Messy, and Merry Christmas, everybody. See you later— (Before he gets to front door, Karl throws piece of fire wood between Mike's legs. Mike stumbles, falls against door with loud crash. All watch but do not move. Baby cries, suddenly and loud as curtain falls on Scene 2)

ᴥ ACT II, SCENE 3 ᴥ

While curtain is falling, baby's cries gradually change to persistent and increasingly loud 'space noises/music.' A very elaborately furnished and decorated chair (throne) standing on a platform is pulled (or lowered) onto stage in front of curtain. Above the seat in a steeple-like enclosure hangs a bell that keeps swinging after chair has come to rest. The back of the chair resembles elaborate cabinet doors covering a long mirror. Short pause with spotlights on throne, very bright in contrast to dark curtain. Enter Lucifer dressed in tight-fitting black suit with a few glittering decorations and ornaments. Crown on his head. He carries a ledgerlike heavily bound book for reading and writing.

LUCIFER: (Short pause) My, my—what a nasty thing to do, Karl. Ghastly, I'd venture—make poor Mike trip and fall like that. Reverting to your former habits, Karl? Some of your former life, perhaps? Violence? (Rubs his hands) On Christmas Eve? My, my. (Opens ledger, reads) Let me see—where are we? Ah, yes. Here we are—December—our special month—let me see—December 22—35 Cottage Row in Loweville—pains, false alarm—

FRANK E. SCHACHT

no baby. December 23—ditto—no baby. December
24—that's today, right? (Checks with elaborate
computer watch) Right. (He steps to the back of
throne, takes key that hangs from gold chain
around his neck. Speaks to audience) Perhaps you
are surprised that we have books—have books
and read from them, spirits that we are,
essentially, and most of the time—(Pause, he
opens doors in back of chair with his key, looks at
himself in mirror, appropriate actions) I—I am
Lucifer, by the way, I always travel elaborately—
enter and leave—on this, my con-vey-ance, my
car, as you would say. Very convenient, and very
efficient. Runs on energy—cosmic energy—no
pollution, no noise—you ought to try it one day—
if your potentates will let you. (Pause, action
before mirror) I myself am a potentate, sort of,
fallen—yes, but never quite forgotten—Some refer
to me as the 'Prince of Darkness'—a totally
unfounded name because my home is bright and
aglow with mighty fires. Again, no smoke, and no
refueling, a little like your new nuclear power—
my—how close you _are_ getting to our secrets.
(Pause, he steps away from mirror, closes doors,
puts key back inside his suit) Yes, (Opens ledger)
we do have books. We read and we write. (Writes)
Perhaps—you are—jealous? You envy us because
we read and write? Yes? You shouldn't. You

39

have _your_ books, especially those you call _scriptures_—written books. You have your holy books, and we have ours. So there. (Pause) Difference is—you _read_ from yours while we _write_ ours. You read and accept. We write and create— new books every year—new holy books for every month, day. Diaries, sort of—di-a-ries. (Pause) You receive—we give. (Pause) Let me see—where was I? Ah yes, December 24. (Checks watch) The visitors should have arrived by now. (Peers at and through curtain) They have—good. (Checks) Baby born. (Writes) Always check, check and recheck. (Turns several pages, pause) Another matter where we are superior, I think—we can change from spirit into matter, anytime we want to. Now we are spirits, now creatures. (Playacts) Now you see us—(Disappears briefly behind curtain) I tell you, and you can trust me on this— (Pause, he sits on throne—grandly) Even the Lord cannot do this. (Pause) Tried it once—his grand experiment for mankind. Ended in terrible disaster—agony, torture, crucifixion (Acts out)—horrible. (Pause) But he will keep on trying, I guess. He will. He must. (Pause) And we—we must be on guard, always on guard. Always check and recheck. (Opens ledger, briefly) Now—as I said—we spirits can do this all the time—take on the flesh—with all its tribulations. Just watch— (He rings bell

above his seat, twice. Enter, in the most spectacular
and silent way possible, Samiel and Uriel. Both
are dressed like Lucifer, but with fewer
decorations and no crowns)

S/U: You belled, sir. (Pause)

LUCIFER: Yes, I did, indeed—Where have you been? —I told
you time and again, you shouldn't leave me alone
so long. I think too much when I am by myself. I—
phi-lo-sop-hize—horrible. (Shakes himself, gets
up and steps from throne)

SAMIEL: Sorry, sir. December, you know, very busy time
for us—

URIEL: Very busy.

LUCIFER: Yes, I know. I know (Reads from ledger) And very
successful, too. (To audience) We have made them
so busy this month, made them and kept them
busy—buying gifts, buying and selling business
this, business that, parties, trees, decorations,
lights, eating, drinking (All playact, ad-lib) So
busy—we've almost buried them under their
activities, and almost erased—wiped out, almost,
that—that feast at the end of the month, (To S/J)
haven't we? Took us nearly 2000 years—but now
we're almost there, aren't we?

S/U: We are, sir—almost—yes.

LUCIFER: (Back to throne) But tell me—how are things
going on Cottage Row?—35 Cottage Row, in
Loweville. The visitors, the baby—they have not

arrived—not yet, I believe—

SAMIEL: Oh yes, they have, sir.

URIEL: Indeed, they have—

SAMIEL: As planned, sir—almost.

URIEL: Almost—

LUCIFER: Almost? How—almost?

SAMIEL: He didn't put the money in the envelope—

LUCIFER: Who didn't—in whose envelope?

SAMIEL: Karl—*your* Karl Litus—he didn't put the cash into Mike Balser's envelope, as you had suggested in the original plan—

LUCIFER: And the woman? Dolores Messenger—our Messy?

SAMIEL: Oh—her—he gave *her* the money, all right, but not to *him*, not to Mike Balser.

URIEL: The prejudiced, godforsaken hypocrite—

SAMIEL: Shut up, Urie—

LUCIFER: Quiet, you two. (Pause) So—no money, no cash for Balser. Well—I am damned. (Pause) That fool, oh that double-living fool, Karl Litus-*my* Karl—

S/U: *Your* Karl—

LUCIFER: (Angry) It's that *will* of theirs, that damned free will. Ruins everything, everything ever created— ruined by that free *will*. (To himself) I should know— (Opens mirror) Some day—and if it takes billennia—some day when I am admitted to Court again, I must discuss this matter with the Lord— this damned free will—his, and mine, and ours, and everybody's. (Pause, locks mirror, then

speaks to S/U) So—no money for Balser. And
what did *you* do? How did *you* manage?

SAMIEL: (Grandly) Well, sir, I changed into the winter
wind (Playacts) temporarily, and I followed him
all the way—

URIEL: (Interrupting) As we figured it, sir, the woman,
Messy, she would get here on her own, on account
of money, the 500 dollars she got from Karl, like
you suggested, sir, and with which she bought
herself a fur coat, a Christmas rabbit fur coat, and
boots to go with it—

SAMIEL: (Pushes Uriel aside) I figured, sir, she would want
more where *that* came from and come to Cottage
Row, all right. And it worked, sir. She got here,
walked all the way, she did—

LUCIFER: (To himself) Liar—she took a taxi—probably
another one of Karl's hu-man-i-tar-i-an ideas—
(To S/U) But Balser, how about him?

SAMIEL: Like I said—I trailed him all the way, practically
blew him here. And he got here, too. With the
bottle, of course.

LUCIFER: Ah yes, the bottle, of course. Brilliant idea I gave
to Karl—bottle a for the baby, but a gin bottle—
(Laughs) Bottle, in one form or another, gets them
all the time, from birth to death— (To Samiel) Best
gin, I hope? Beefeater?

SAMIEL: Paregoric.

LUCIFER: What did you say?

SAMIEL: Paregoric, sir. Another thing that went wrong. Instead of gin, Karl— 'your Karl' put paregoric into the bottle—

LUCIFER: Not for the baby—

SAMIEL: For the baby.

LUCIFER: (Fake anger, alarm) But—if they give it to the baby, it will kill him. No—not paregoric, not un-di-lu-ted, not to a newborn, innocent baby— (Sits down, cries) Well—I'm damned again, damned and doubled damned. Just wait till the season is over, Karl, and we have more time. We'll take care of you, just wait—

SAMIEL: Right, sir—just wait. (Pause)

LUCIFER: (Quieter, to Uriel) And the boy? How's the boy?

URIEL: (Steps forward, rubs his hands) He's on the way, sir. The boy is on the way.

LUCIFER: On the way?

URIEL: To Cottage Row, sir.

LUCIFER: (Getting louder and louder. Gets up, walks) To Cottage Row. (Mimics) And you are here? The boy's on his way and you are not with him? You let him out of your sight?

URIEL: I stayed with him. Through snow and hail and wind and bitter cold. (Shivers violently) I stayed with him, sir. You don't seem to realize how much this cold hurts us, coming from the climate we are used to. (Pause) But, sir, I swear it, I swear it on the di-a-ry: stayed with him—until you belled—twice.

LUCIFER: (Thundering) I belled—twice—right—and now
I'm telling you: get back on the job, you shivering
jerk. Get back—and stay with the boy, you hear?
(Uriel gradually slinks away) Stay with him until
he gets there, you understand? The boy—he has
the key. You hear me? You understand? The key—
the key—the boy has the key. Make sure he gets
here—make doubly sure. (Uriel exits) I called
him—of course, I did. (Paces up and down) I have
my rights, too. (Pause) The mal-e-dict hell of it.
The double-damned, maledict hell of it—as if I
didn't have enough trouble with man—and now
my own people, too. Why can't _they_ think, for
once? Why don't _they_ use a little of that —that free
will? (Sits, pause)

SAMIEL: Free will, yes, sir—free will.

LUCIFER: And that's all that went wrong? Just that—the
money and the gin? That's all?

SAMIEL: (Frightened) Sir—there is the woman, too.

LUCIFER: Woman? What woman?

SAMIEL: Elizabeth—they call her Malchen.

LUCIFER: Malchen? Elizabeth? Don't know her. Let me see.
(Goes to curtain, looks at it for a while) No—don't
know her. None of my people, anyhow—
(to audience) And I thought we had dealt with
that problem—woman—a long, long time ago.
Wasn't she the first creature we had success with?
The first, ever? (Goes to throne, opens up seat,

takes out another old volume) Let me see. (Reads)
Right—woman—Eve—first, ever—

SAMIEL: Except for the snake, sir—the snake, remember?

LUCIFER: Oh-shut up, you sniveling knave. You weren't
even born yet—

SAMIEL: I didn't have to be—I—was—cre-a-ted, same as
you, sir—

LUCIFER: Yes, yes, you already told me. (Gets up, paces)
How I distrust people with more than one name,
distrust and dislike them—with the trillions of
names we have to deal with, enough to burst one's
brain with just one name for each. (Opens ledger,
writes) Another thing I _must_ discuss with _him_
(Gesture) Names—people's names. Would be
much easier if all had just numbers—like 00 61 54
93 48 75 09—would be much easier. And more
exact too, like telephone numbers—or what they
now call 'social security' (Grunt. To Samiel)
Malchen, you said?

SAMIEL: No, sir—Elizabeth, alias Malchen. You can see
her—over there, by the stove. (Both go to curtain)
She's the one who does all the cooking. (Both nod
in agreement) You see, sir, this woman, this
Mal-chen—she has this theory, this — idea. I don't
like it all. It doesn't fit into our plans, not any of
them— Worse yet, she not only thinks—she acts.
Not just theory—practice as well.

LUCIFER: (Is back on his throne, writing and only half

listening) What theory? What idea?

SAMIEL: (Grandly) The theory, sir, that in some way the 'good' —she calls it that but sometimes gets it mixed up with 'god' (Shivers)—that in some way the good she thinks about can become reality through words and actions—

LUCIFER: (Excited) What did you say? An idea, a word— become reality through action? Haven't we heard this before, somewhere? This woman, this Mal-chen—she's becoming a problem, a dangerous problem. Just wait, lady, till the season is over. (Both walk back and forth)

SAMIEL: I really don't understand it myself, sir. All I know is that she always seems to foul up our plans, our work. Just by being there, just by doing what she does—

LUCIFER: And—you haven't done anything about it?

SAMIEL: Oh yes, sir. I have. Been following her, been listening. She lives alone, you know, and some times I hear her talking to herself—thinking out loud, sort of. Phi-lo-sop-hize—if you know what I mean, really.

LUCIFER: Well—you Samiel, you keep your eye on this person, you hear? Both eyes. And your ears open. Both ears. I must know more about this—theory— sounds like theft—grand lar-ce-ny—she's stealing, stealing from us. (To Samiel) You keep her covered. You brought two people to the cottage safely—

good boy. Now, deal with that woman, too.
(Samiel slowly goes off with bows, 'yes sirs,' etc.)
And also make sure (Very loud), doubly sure that
Ur-i-el takes care of the boy. (Echo: 'the boy') He is
the key. (Echo: 'the key') (Echoes gradually
change to previous space noises/music. They are
getting louder and louder as Lucifer gets back on
throne and is pulled (or lifted) off stage)

INTERMISSION

✣ ACT III, SCENE 1 ✣

An hour later, toward evening of the same day. Living room at 35 Cottage Row, as in ACT I. Lights have been turned on the table near the stove. Mike is sitting in rocking chair. 'Messy' is checking the bandage on his head.

DOLORES: That was a nasty fall, Mike. But you won't die from it. There—keep that bandage on for a day or two. Does it hurt?

MIKE: It does, but not too much. I must have tripped, I guess—tripped over something, right?

DOLORES: Yes, a piece of firewood on the floor. You knocked yourself out for a while. Have any dreams?

MIKE: (Tries to get up, moans, touches his head, falls back into chair) I did. But—not the kind I could tell _you_ about. Another thing I took with me from my cell: my dreams. They come to me, keep coming. They overwhelm me, like a giant movie screen wrapped all around me. (Shakes his head, moans) Where is everybody?

DOLORES: The man, Karl, and the woman, Malchen, are outside, somewhere. Looking for more firewood, I guess the storm must have knocked out some the power lines. And the furnace is almost out.

49

MIKE: But—wasn't there a young couple, too?

DOLORES: Of course. They live here. Are in the back room
now trying to get some sleep. The baby, too. Has
been some day for all of them. And for us.
(Gets busy working on stove, table, etc.)

MIKE: (Watches her for a while. Then gets up slowly)
That leaves us, here, alone.

DOLORES: With our letters—and those funny gifts.

MIKE: (Feeling his head) God—it's like another dream,
something that hits you from the outside, sort of—

DOLORES: Like a front door, maybe—

MIKE: And now—it's all coming back to me. (Looks at
his watch) Wonder how long we'll have to wait.
It's getting late.

DOLORES: Might be some time. Things move slowly in
the woods.

MIKE: (Irritated, gets up again) I'm beginning to think
it's all a big hoax. Somebody's silly idea—like an
experiment, or some kind of plot. Or just a damn
joke. And I fell for it. (Pause)

DOLORES: That's right. You did. But you did get that
letter, right?

MIKE: Right?

DOLORES: So did I. (She pulls a chair next to the rocker, and
both sit down) And there was a—present in the
letter, right?

MIKE: (Loud) No, not in it—_with_ it. In a separate package. A bottle, which I handed over to them. Some

stupid joke—paregoric.

DOLORES: And you got no money? No cash?

MIKE: (Sharply) I didn't. But _you_ did. I remember.

DOLORES: That's right. And I spent it all on clothes, and to get out here. Stupid of me, really. (Gets up and walks around) How are we going to get back to the city now? And when?

MIKE: (Louder) Not before I get _my_ present too, you hear—

DOLORES: Okay, okay—don't holler at me. I'm in the same boat. Besides—I want to be your friend. (Pause) Reminds me—I had a present to hand over, too. Never did—there was a little—complication. (Mike does not pay attention) Wonder what it could be. Here it is. Here is the envelope (Takes it from her purse) Wonder what's in it.

MIKE: (Still loud) We—let's open it. Let's see. Maybe more money.

DOLORES: (Shakes envelope next to her ear) No—sorry, no money. It sort of rattles inside, like sand, or something.

MIKE: Stop acting like a kid on Christmas morning, will you? Open it up.

DOLORES: Okay, if you say so. What the hell— No, I guess I'd rather not. Deal is a deal.

MIKE: (Looks at her, shakes head) Strange—it's still like—like a dream—

DOLORES: What?

MIKE: (Softly) How two people like you and I can get
         together—never seen each other before, never
         met. And suddenly—we have so many things in
         common—same letters, gifts—damn them, damn
         the words even—and all seems nothing more than
         a dream.

DOLORES: (Equally soft) But when we get back, we'll get
         together again, maybe. (Pause) And maybe the
         dream will become reality. Some of it anyhow.
         We'll have things to talk about.

MIKE: We sure do. Guess we'd better start off now. (Gets
         up and walks slowly to table) Steady now. (Holds
         out his hand) Give me your hand, girl. Want to
         walk over to the table. It's warmer there.
         (Dolores helps)

DOLORES: You have a strong grip, Mike.
         (Both sit down at table)

MIKE: (Looks at hands, then at Dolores) Strong—, too
         strong, I'm afraid—

DOLORES: What do you mean?

MIKE: (Looks at her, shakes his head) Oh, nothing,
         nothing at all. (Looks at his hands again) Wish I
         was strong up here, too. (Points to his head)
         Wouldn't have fallen for this—this fake promise in
         the letter. Could have sold that bottle of—
         paregoric—to somebody—_somebody'd_ pay me
         cash for it. (Looks at Dolores) Wonder if there's
         somebody else—

DOLORES: What do you mean?

MIKE: (Irritated) What do I mean? What do I mean?— I
mean—if there's somebody else who got a letter—
fake promise—that's what I mean.

DOLORES: Okay, okay. I hear—don't shout. You'll bust your
bandage— (While she is saying this, there's the
noise of pieces of wood being thrown outside)
There's somebody now, in any case.
(Goes to window, looks out)

MIKE: Who is it?

DOLORES: Somebody's bringing more wood.

MIKE: The man and the woman? Karl and—Malchen?

DOLORES: No—there's—there's—three of them. Looks like
there's three men—

MIKE: I thought there might be somebody else, yet.
Didn't I tell you? (Gets up slowly) I'll see
for myself—

DOLORES: You'd better stay where you are, in your
condition. You'd better save your strength for
later. We still have to get back, you know. (Half
pushes Mike back into his chair. He pushes her
hand away, roughly, but sits down again. She goes
to door, unlocks and opens it. Wind noises, snow.
Just then, bedroom door opens. Enter Joe and
Mary with baby)

JOE: (Rubs his hands) Warmer in here. Thanks for
keeping the fire going. Warmer in here. We heard
somebody bringing more wood. (Sits at table)

Had a good rest, all three of us. (Mary sits down next to him)

MARY: Got to get some food ready now. Let me see what's left. (Gets up)

DOLORES: I still got that present for you. Here— (Gives envelope to Mary) You open it. It's for you—

MARY: (Sits down again) I still can't believe it. But— thank you. (She takes envelope, opens it, sniffs at contents) Looks like—I don't know—like small stones. Sand or small stones, or something. (Shakes her head, hands envelope to Joe) What is it? Do you know, Joe?

JOE: (After short pause) It's—it's—incense. Here— (Pours some of the contents on saucer. Gets a candle, lights it, then burns some of the incense)

DOLORES: Well—I'll be damned. This is getting spookier the darker it gets outside. Wonder what will be next. (All sit around table, look at candle and burning incense. Suddenly, front door is pushed open, enter Karl and Malchen with pot and food containers)

MIKE: (Gets up) So there you are. About time. Got the stuff—whatever it might be?

KARL: We got some food—

DOLORES: And more wood, too. I saw you, just a little while ago—

KARL: No. We didn't bring any more wood. Just food. Heated up in Malchen's kitchen. Good stuff. Brought it over in the car—

MALCHEN: Beef stew, homemade. Always keep some in the
refrigerator. Just in case. Always better warmed
up. So sit down, everybody. We'll eat, then we'll
talk. Got some pudding too, for dessert—

DOLORES: (Stubborn) But—I saw you outside. I did. Just a
little while ago. You were on the porch, unloading
some wood. (Helps Malchen with table, food, etc.)

KARL: I saw the new woodpile, too. But _we_ didn't bring it.

MALCHEN: Never mind now. Never mind the wood. Table
all set now? Can we start?

KARL: (Quiet and firm) Set one more place,
Malchen, please.

DOLORES: One more? For whom?

KARL: There are—three of you. Three. One still to come.
You'll see. One more place, please, Malchen.
(Malchen sets one more place)

DOLORES: (Confused) Didn't I tell you—three—I saw three
outside—bringing wood?

MIKE: Oh—stop your whining. _I_ told _you_ there might be
another—Now—let's eat. (Falls to his food. Others
start to eat. Baby begins soft crying. Pause,
curtain)

⚔ ACT III, SCENE 2 ⚕

In front of curtain. Space music mixed with wind, snow, etc. Enter from left a young man, about 17, poorly dressed, shivering in the cold. He gropes and staggers as if he is making his way from tree to tree. As he gets to middle of stage, he pulls something from his jacket pocket, looks at it, shakes his head, puts it back and continues his slow walk. Just then, main curtain is raised and a special, translucent curtain is lowering behind which in growing light the main part of the stage becomes gradually visible. Young man, meanwhile, looks more and more confused and has more and more trouble staying on his feet. Behind him, entering from left, a dark figure appears that keeps same distance as both gradually move to right side of stage. Louder space music as second curtain opens and lights go up on a main part of stage.

KARL: (Between bites) Good food.

JOE: Very good. Thanks for bringing it over. Haven't eaten this much for some time. —Mary, isn't that the baby crying?

MARY: I just put him to bed. Not time for him. Just fed, don't you remember? (All are silent while wind noises and baby's cries are becoming louder)

KARL: Now that we've had our food and we all
feel better—

MIKE: I'll feel better when I get what I came for. Now,
give me that damn—gift, and then I'll get back to
the city. (To Dolores) You're coming too, right?
Only—I don't know how we'll get there. (Gets up)

MALCHEN: I'll take you in my car. Don't worry about it.
Here—have some of the pudding. Good— has
brandy in it. Have some. Don't rush off right now.

KARL: And let me explain about that gift you're asking
about all the time—

MIKE: You'd better—(Passes plate to Malchen,
sits down)

KARL: (Pushes his chair back, leans back in it, waits until
everybody is served) It was all my doing. I am
responsible. I sent you the letters.

MIKE: I thought so—all along. (To Dolores) Never trusted
this man, from the first time I saw him. (Loud)
Dragging us out here—nobodies into nowhere
land— (Dolores makes sign to him to keep quiet)

KARL: I couldn't foresee the weather, of course. I couldn't
possibly. I am sorry. And I'm worrying about the
other one—

DOLORES: The other one?

KARL: (Holds everybody's attention for the next few
minutes. Speaks slowly at first, then more clearly
and firmly) The other one—anyhow—two out of
three isn't so bad—and he might get here yet.

Now, listen to me for just a few minutes. Listen.
You're going to hear a strange story, and perhaps
you're listening to a strange man. (Pause) I don't
know exactly how these ideas come to me—how
they have kept coming ever since I was young, a
boy—suddenly, somebody or something was
there to tell me what to do. Some—power that
comes and tidies up my own wishes in neat
packages and then tells me what to do with them.
Strange things—When I was a boy, strange and
often stupid things. And there was nobody else to
tell me right from wrong—

DOLORES: (Sympathetically) You were alone—no home?

KARL: (Looks at her. Nods) In a way, yes. My parents
split up. They never got along. Hated each other's
sight. Fought all day long—anyhow—these
voices—I listened to them and got involved in
crazy things: street fights, burglaries, knifings
drinking. Ended up in prison when I was barely
eighteen—

MIKE: (Loud and sneering but not malicious)
Don't tell me—

KARL: I did. (Speaks earnestly, at times emotionally) And
I had a lot of time to think and learn. (Excited as if
trying to convince himself) I began to fight these—
voices. I had it out with them. Told them to—to
keep their shit asses shut—they got me into all this
trouble, and I told them to just shut up. (Pause,
more quietly) It took a long time, and the prison

was a tight, tough place. Not many temptations there. Not much choice except to grow straight or rot away inside. For a while I was winning. Thought I was, anyhow, I learned a trade, too. Carpentry—woodworking.

JOE: You—a carpenter, too? (Pause) Mary, you'd better look after the baby. He keeps on crying—

MARY: Don't worry about him. Just fed him. Crying sounds okay. Probably does him good—

MALCHEN: Shows he is alive and healthy—
More pudding, anybody?

KARL: When I got out, I decided to start all over, new town, new life. I was still young then, you know. First I got my own carpenter shop, then started in a small woodworking plant in the city. I was lucky. Worked hard. Worked my way up. After years, I bought up this plant, here in the country. Comes with the cottages which I'm renting out. You know the rest—

JOE: You—you mean—you are the boss?

KARL: Wood in winter, too. A roof, stove, beds, some furniture, steady work, a family. Some of the good things in life. Makes some people satisfied, even happy—

MIKE: (Shakes his head) Sounds like fairy tales to me— but perhaps—you have a point, mister. But tell me, what does this have to do with us—the letters, the presents—

KARL: (Very earnestly) It was a—test. I wanted to see if it
        works on other people, too. I wanted to learn—if
        others might hear—voices too. Hear them and
        follow them.

DOLORES: Voices?

KARL: Yes—I'm still hearing them sometimes. After all
        these years. They still tell me what to do, and how
        to do it. Crazy ideas, some of them at least—

DOLORES: Like writing letters to strangers, maybe?

KARL: Yes. Exactly. (Pause) The idea came to me last
        September—after this young couple answered my
        ad and moved in here from the city. The idea
        was—to pick three people whom I'd never seen or
        met before—one still in prison, a woman, and a
        boy in his teens—

MALCHEN: And where is the boy?

KARL: Don't know. Maybe he didn't get the letter.
        Maybe. (Pause) It was a test, you see. Some pass,
        some fail—

MIKE: (Impatient) And then?

KARL: Then I did a lot of research, did a lot of walking
        and talking. Took me weeks, and it was hard
        work, especially in your case, Mike. Anyhow—I
        finally sent off the letters, told the three people
        what to do, gave them directions, made them a
        promise to give them some—incentive, some
        motive you might say—

MALCHEN: Doesn't sound crazy to me. Unusual, yes, but

not crazy. (Pause)

KARL: Thanks. (Pause) As I explained to you—it wasn't really _my_ idea, alone. Somebody put it into my head—

MALCHEN: But—it was a success. Two out of three are here, two made it—

KARL: (After a pause) Yes. You're right. Two are here. Except—at first—it was really a crazy idea. Like— your present, Mike, the one you brought—it was supposed to be a —bottle of gin.
(Pause, then laughter)

MIKE: Gin—for a newborn baby. Crazy—you're right.

KARL: So—I changed the contents of the bottle. You know the rest—

MIKE: I know. You wanted to make sure I didn't drink the stuff on the way, didn't you? Paregoric— drugs, cheap stuff. (Pause) Mary—you know how to use this—medicine? It's very strong—

DOLORES: Maybe you can try it out on yourself first. In case you get the runs—after all you've eaten.
(Loud laughter)

KARL: And you'll get your gift too. Don't worry. (Baby cries louder from bedroom)

JOE: (Nervous) Mary—for God's sake, take care of the baby. The noise makes me nervous. Maybe he needs changing. You know, in the back. (Playacts) Want me to go and do it? (Laughter)

MARY: No. I will do it. Right away. I want to hear the rest

of this strange story. So—it was a test? For all of
us? How did we get involved? Joe and me?

KARL: You were going to have a baby. My foreman told
me after your interview. The baby would come at
about the right time—

MARY: But just suppose—he was not on time. Suppose he
was early, or late—

KARL: I took my chances. It was a test. You always take
chances in tests. (To Dolores) As for you—

DOLORES: Don't say it. I know it already. You picked me, a
woman—well-known in certain parts of town,
with a certain reputation—

MIKE: (Excited, angry) Don't you say it either, Messy—
don't spell it out for him—don't punish yourself.
Come on, let's get out of here. I'm leaving (To
Karl), leaving this place, and especially you and
your—silly—tests. (Bitter) Before you give tests,
mister, you got to do a little teaching. I _mean_, real
teaching, not just—some letter with instructions.
Did _you_ do _your_ teaching, mister? Before _your_ test?
No, you didn't. It was a fake, like your gift, a fake.
(Very loud) All you ever want to do is—play
god—with me and with all these people too. Play
god. (Pause) Well, in _your_ kind of heaven—there's
no place for me. I'm leaving. (To Dolores) Coming?

DOLORES: No—not yet, Mike. (To Karl) So you wanted to
know if I listened—to advice? To voices? Read
letters? From a stranger? You put me to the test?

Well—you found out. I did read, I did listen. The only thing I am sorry about is that I obeyed you and spent all the money. But—I'm here. So, what's next? (To Mike) I guess you're right, we better— (Loud baby noises from bedroom. Mary gets up quickly. Just as she reaches bedroom door, there's a loud crash in front of main door. Then main door is pushed open from outside by Henry who half staggers, half falls inside. He is a boy of about 16, poorly dressed, especially for winter storms. After entering, he lies on his chest and face for a few seconds while everybody stares at him)

KARL: The boy—oh my God—he got here, he's here— (Jumps up) Come on, help me, somebody. Let's put him on the sofa next to the stove. My God, he's half frozen. Get some blankets, some hot food, maybe. Come on, let's go.
(Everybody suddenly wakes up and starts helping Karl. Commotion)

MIKE: Easy, easy there, you guys—At least, he's still breathing, still alive. Take it easy, or we'll kill him yet—

KARL: You, Mike and Dolores—you take care of him. I'll bring in more wood from the porch (Puts on hat and coat while Mike and Dolores bend over Henry. While Karl leaves, curtain is lowered, lights go out, space noises and music begin again. No intermission)

⊰ ACT IV, SCENE 1 ⊱

After curtain has fallen and lights are out completely, there is a short pause for music, wind noises, etc. Then lights come on slowly. On stage right Karl can be seen picking up scraps of wood. On stage left, Lucifer wearing same costume but with coat and hood over his crown. He too picks up wood, mimics Karl for a little while.

LUCIFER: (Shivering, rubbing his hands) Brrr—this idea of playing the part of men is—brilliant. And it must be pleasant, too—in the South Seas. (Pause) But around here, it's too cold. Brrr—cold as a comet. (Looks at Karl, mimics) Right now, I wish I was where I belong. But tonight, in this part of the world—(Deep sigh) This night is always the most difficult for our kind of work. (Walks up and down, rubs hands repeatedly) Becoming more difficult, it seems. More difficult by the century. (Pause) Now—if I were really a man, like brother Karl over there, I'd say it's—old age. It's not that things are getting more difficult—but that _we_ are getting more difficult. (Pause) Take that man, for example, (To audience) that wood-gatherer, the external doer, Karl Litus. He's been on our payroll for years now, ever since he was a boy. We tried to cash in on his miserable childhood. Been dealing him some of our best cards, giving him some of our best ideas. And for years it worked, beautifully. No sweat. (Pause) But lately? Today? No sir. Has to have it his way. More and more—his way. I think I'll have another talk with him. (To himself) That's right, Luci, take time out. After all, time means nothing to us, does it? (He brushes snow off his coat, kicks wood over to side of stage, talks to audience) That's one thing we can still bank on—time. We are _above_ it. Even produce it. You say 'time is money,' right—well—_you_ make money, _we_ make time (He reaches under his coat and pulls out ledger which he opens. Briefly reads and writes in it, while spotlight shifts to Karl)

KARL: The woods are getting cold and deep. (Pause) I can hardly see the wood I'm supposed to pick. (Straightens up) I'm really getting tired of wood-picking. And I wish I hadn't changed the contents of that bottle. Could go back inside and get a little gin. Would taste good, right now. (Pause) First ideas, best ideas—

SAMIEL: (Arrives suddenly, if possible from above stage. Dressed like Lucifer) So—why did you change? It was a good plan—a baby bottle filled with gin—

KARL: (To himself) Why did I change? Changed my mind, I guess—thought the better of it—

SAMIEL: (Mimics) The better—the better. That's all you're ever thinking about, now that you're getting older? Right? The older—the better?

KARL: (To Samiel) And what are you bitching about? I did plenty of jobs for _you_ when I was young, didn't I? High time I thought more about myself— besides—times change and we change with them.

LUCIFER: (Who has worked his way over to stage right) We don't—and time doesn't change for us. In fact (Grandly) time doesn't even exist for us.

SAMIEL: (To himself and audience) The liar. Every year, at this time, he gets the shakes Because of the time of year it is. I know. (Pretends to pick up wood)

KARL: (To Lucifer) And who are _you_? And who _asked_ you?

SAMIEL: (To Karl) He's the boss. (Pause) So, you'd better show a little respect, or else—we'll burn your ears off.

KARL: Right now, a little fire wouldn't be such a bad idea—

SAMIEL: (Produces a lighter, sudden big flame) Big mouth, eh? Want me to do it to him, boss? (Holds flame close to Karl's face)

LUCIFER: No, leave him alone. He has served. (To himself) And he will serve again—

KARL: Maybe. (Bends down, goes back to picking up wood)

LUCIFER: (Produces his own lighter, or equivalent, lights it,

places it in front of him, sits down with ledger,
rubs his hands) Maybe — maybe. (Sighs) How
complicated the earth has become—all because
they still have their free will. And they're ornery.
Ornery and stubborn, that's what they are.
(Writes) They just won't do what they're told.
Must discuss this problem with the big boss—
whenever—if at all. (Signs, closes ledger, tosses it
to Samiel) Here, Sam—_you_ write it down, too.
Make a note of it, Sam—(Pause) Why do they
have their free will? And why are they so ornery?
Got that, Sam?

SAMIEL: (Has caught ledger, takes off gloves, writes) Yes,
boss. I got it.

LUCIFER: (Gets up, walks) As if I didn't know the answer
already. 'It's all _your_ fault,' he will holler. (Mimics)
'I made them _free_ —and you made them _ornery_.
(Echoes: free—ornery) It's all _your_ fault—ever
since you started to crawl on your belly, and to
make like a snake.' (Playacts) And I will say: 'Yes
sir, but I was following orders. I did— (Sighs)

SAMIEL: (To himself and audience) Lucifer—he was never
told to crawl, never. He wanted to—

LUCIFER: (Sharply) Sam—come over here, Sam—

SAMIEL: Yes, boss— (Walks carefully toward Lucifer)

LUCIFER: (Sits near his lighter. Samiel and Karl listen.
Remember how much simpler things used to be?

SAMIEL: Yes, boss, much simpler. (Closer to Lucifer)

Lucifer: Remember—way back, years ago, like 2000
years—(Samiel turns pages in ledger) Remember
when we sent those three men off—after that star?
And how they marched and marched, day and
night? No sweat. (Laugh) And how they just
followed orders and delivered their gifts. (To Karl)
And there was not question of—change—you
hear?— (Karl holds hands over flame) And then—
we almost got that—that baby thrown into the
bargain, too— Remember? (Pause)

Samiel: I remember. (Rubs his hands) We almost did get
that baby. If it hadn't been for our blasted com-
pe-ti-tion—for some creep do-good-er an-gel—

Lucifer: Who told them not to squeal.

Samiel: And they didn't. And con-se-quent-ly—the killers
didn't find the baby—

Lucifer: (Clear, angry) No—his parents hid him—and then
he lived, for another 30 years or so, anyhow.

Samiel: But still, boss, hundreds of other kids died—
hundreds of little kids, for one. Not too bad, is it?
(Rubs his hands over flame)

Lucifer: No, not too bad. But—the point is—it wasn't the
three men's idea to switch plans. It was that—do-
gooder angel's idea. Right? (To Karl) But
nowadays—we can't count on _anybody_, right?
(Karl shakes his head. Moves away from flame)

Samiel: There's still that other kid, boss. The boy,
remember?

LUCIFER: The boy. The boy. I almost forgot. (Snaps his
  fingers. Uriel enters, from above, if possible)
URIEL: Yes, boss—you snapped?
LUCIFER: Where's the boy, Uriel? The boy?
URIEL: The boy? Oh-he got there, okay. I saw to it, I did.
  Half frozen, but he got there. (Moves to flame,
  rubs hands) I'm damn near half frozen myself—
  (To Samiel) What's he trying to do to us? Get rid
  of us, huh? Can't burn us, so he's trying to freeze
  us, huh?
LUCIFER: And my plan? Did it work?
URIEL: (Gets up, shrugs) I tried to make it work, boss— I
  did, honest—I tried to get him to sell the thing,
  and buy himself some food or at least a coat—in
  this weather, boss—I mean, God— (Samiel kicks
  his shin) I even tried to get him into a nice warm
  pawnshop—nice place with pinball machines—
  (Demonstrates) It didn't work, boss. Nothing did.
  Too stubborn, the young cuss.
  (Goes back to flame)
LUCIFER: So—there we are again—
URIEL: He would rather freeze his fingers off his hand,
  one by one (Playacts) 'Got this watch to deliver,'
  he kept mumbling. 'Made up my mind, promised
  I'd deliver it—got to keep the promise'— (Pause)
  The fool—never made a promise, except to
  himself—Gold watch, too. Real gold. Could have
  gotten 300 for it, 400, 500—the price of gold keeps

going up so fast, you know.

SAMIEL: Or—he could have sold it, and bought a cheap
watch instead. He could have both, the money
and a watch, the fool. Right, boss?

LUCIFER: (Sharp and loud, to Karl) It was your fault. It was
all _your_ fault.

KARL: That's right. I seem to have picked the wrong guy.

LUCIFER: And—after you picked him so carefully, you said.
After you had watched him, gone to the city
several times, observed him—

KARL: That's right, but—

SAMIEL: (Viciously) But—you're going to pay—that will be
your 'but', mister. Right, boss? (Holds lighter close
to Karl's face)

LUCIFER: Leave him alone for now. Let's first see what
really happened to the boy. We may have a chance
with him yet.

⚔ ACT IV, SCENE 2 ⚔

After curtain rises lights switch from front to center and backstage. All are still sitting around the table, including Henry who is eating slowly.

DOLORES: So, here you are. Almost finished your food. Are you feeling better now? At least you are sitting up.

HENRY: Yes, thank you, much better. Thanks for the food. It was delicious. Really—

MALCHEN: (Gets up and clears plates) 'Hunger is the best cook,' they used to say at home. Old saying— German, I think. Here, have some of the pudding, too.

MIKE: Number three you are, eh?

HENRY: How's that?

DOLORES: Easy—there's Mike, number one. I am number two, and now you—number three.

HENRY: (Between mouthfuls of food) Number three, you said? Funny—

MIKE: You can say that again. Have been sitting here for hours, all afternoon. It's been getting darker and colder outside, and here we are—waiting, still waiting. And all we learned, really, is to count to three. (Laughs)

Dolores: (Suddenly very sharp, to Mike) Oh, shut up, will
you. You and your complaining. Makes me sick.
Shut up and let the boy eat. (Milder to Henry)
Finish your dessert. And tell me—what *is* so
funny? The letter? Did you get a letter, too?

Henry: Being number three—me—that's funny.

Dolores: And why is that so funny? Tell us, please.

Henry: (Very deliberately) Well—you always hear about
number one. Everybody wants to be number one,
right? Winner here, winner there, right?

Mike: That's me—

Dolores: Shut up, I told you. And let the boy finish.

Mike: (Gives her long look) Okay, okay. I heard you the
first time. What's the matter with you suddenly?
You become a mother hen, or something? Is that
it? (Dolores stares at him, and he leans back in
his chair)

Henry: Then there's number two. They are supposed to
try harder—

Mike: (Sharp and loud) They sure do. (Dolores gives him
another long look, then moves her chair away
from his and closer to Henry's)

Henry: And I—I'm number three. That's what I find
funny. What does number three ever do?

Mike: Show—show, on the racetrack.

Henry: Show—right. (Laughs) Okay—I show—and here I
am, number three—

DOLORES: And you got a letter, too?

HENRY: I did. A letter, and a present to deliver to 35
        Cottage Row, Loweville. (Takes these items from
        coat, checks address) Both came in the mail this
        week. So this morning I started walking. Here's
        something I can do, I said to myself, for
        somebody. So—I decided to do it.

KARL: You mean—you started walking? And you
        walked here all the way?

HENRY: Well—not _all_ the way.

KARL: And the package that came with the letter? What
        was in it?

HENRY: (Looks at Karl intently) Hold it mister. Don't I
        know you? Didn't we meet in the city, some time
        ago? Didn't you ask me a lot of questions, some
        time back?

MIKE: (Impatient, rude) Yeah—and why are you asking
        about the package? You already know what was
        in it. You sent us ours, mine and Dolores'. And
        you sent him his too, right? (He tries to reach for
        Dolores' hand, but she pushes him back, hard)

HENRY: (After a pause) Yes, there was a small package
        with the letter. The letter said to deliver what was
        inside , so I opened it to see what was inside.
        (Pause)

DOLORES: And?

HENRY: And—here is what I found. (Stretches out his
        hand but keeps his fist closed) This is the right

address? 35 Cottage Row, Loweville? Right?
(Waits and looks around. All nod, etc.) In that
case—here it is. (Opens his fist)

DOLORES: A pocket watch. A gold watch. Very pretty.

MIKE: Let me see it. (He reaches for it, but Henry
quickly closes his fist. Dolores pushes Mike's
hand away)

HENRY: (Holds up watch for all to see) Nice watch. You're
right. Keeps good time, too. But gave me a hard
time, every since I got it—

KARL: How's that?

HENRY: I—I was tempted to—sell it. Sell it, or hawk it, on
the way. Couple of times I was really tempted.
(Pause) Then a guy gave me a lift along Route 80,
you know, the main highway— Well— I felt like
selling it to him—or just giving it to him so that
he'd drive me all the way. (While Henry is talking,
Mike has taken one of the kitchen knives from the
table. He runs his thumb over the edge to test
its sharpness)

MIKE: And—why—didn't you do it?

HENRY: Didn't trust him. That's why. He might have taken
the watch, then told me to get out at the next stop
light. People are like that, sometimes.

KARL: Sometimes. (Pause)

HENRY: Anyhow—I had already made up my mind to bring
this watch here. And here I am. Number three—
show—like you said a little while ago. (Pause)

DOLORES: Show also wins—kind of —

HENRY: (Determined) Now—where's the baby? The letter also says: 'If there is a baby, give the watch to the baby...'

JOE: He's in the bedroom, with his mother.

HENRY: You—the father?

JOE: Yes.

HENRY: Okay then. Here (Puts watch on table to slide it to Joe, but Mike puts his hand on it first. Raises other hand and knife)

MIKE: Just a minute there.

HENRY: Huh? (All watch intently) You—you aren't the baby, exactly. (Forced laughter)

MIKE: I still don't understand. (Pause, then Dolores gets up, wrenches Mike's hand off the watch, puts her own hand on it and moves it over so that it is again in front of Henry)

DOLORES: Of course, you don't. Some people never do.

HENRY: (Puts his hand over watch) Maybe you don't understand. Maybe nobody does. Maybe nobody understands me, either. (Pause) I'm beginning to feel at home here. (Pause, then suddenly very determined) I got very little, you see. Got little to lose, because I own practically nothing. Dropped out of school, too. Just didn't like it anymore. Now, I do odd jobs here and there. If somebody needs me— (Pause) Sometimes I drive my dad's cab—if he lets me. Sometimes I go back home for some of Mom's cooking—

KARL: I know. I understand.

HENRY: (Determined) But every once in a while something—exciting comes up—or somebody. And I make up my mind. And then I do it. (Pause) And it feels good—to have decided and done it. (Pause) Is that so hard to understand? (Looks around table) I do it and I feel good about it. Is that so hard to understand?

MIKE: (Loud, hard laugh) So—that's what it is. That's what you do it for. The decision, right? And then you feel good. Is that all? (Laugh)

HENRY: (Seriously) No, that's not all. Not quite.

MIKE: Well—what else is there? (Stirs in his chair as if getting ready to get up)

HENRY: I learn things—

MIKE: You could have stayed in school for that. (Cold and arrogant) So—what did you learn today, student? Tell us.

HENRY: (Expansively) I learned—how good food tastes if you are really hungry. And that there are people who will take you in and care for you when it's really cold. Strangers—like you people. (Pause) That's what I learned today. (Mike is trying to get up, but Dolores puts her hand on his shoulder and keeps him in his chair. Short struggle between the two. Mike restless, angry) And—here's your watch, mister. Give it to the baby. (Pushes watch

in Joe's direction so that it comes to rest in middle
to table. Mike wrenches free and pushes Dolores
away. He gets up and kicks his chair back into
room. Dolores falls to other side)

MIKE: (Very loud. Harsh words, action) And here's the
knife. (He raises knife high in the air, then slams it
down into table near Dolores. Knife sways for a
while) Here's your knife, Joe—take that too. You
may need it in this place some day. (Pause, the
speaking to all) And here's woman for you.
(Points to knife on table. Follows swaying motion
with his finger) See it—swaying back and forth.
That's woman for you. (Pause) And see the steel,
and the cutting edge? There is woman for you—
and they're all the same. (Pause) Well—enough of
that. I'm leaving. Made up my mind, as our young
number three would say. Where's my coat? My
hat? I'm leaving. (Very upset) A little while back,
this place smelled good. Of food. Now, it smells
stale. It stinks. I'm leaving. So long— (He takes his
coat and hat, puts them on, kicks chair out of the
way, leaves by front door. Pause. Confusion. Then
enter Mary through bedroom door)

MARY: What is it? What's all this noise?

JOE: Here—Mary. Still another gift. Look. The young
man brought a watch for the baby. A gold watch.
Imagine— (Gives her the watch)

KARL: Better pull that knife out of the table, too.

(Joe obeys, takes knife, goes back to bedroom with
Mary. Just before they reach the door, Mary
turns around)

MARY: Thank you. (Pause, with lights on Joe and Mary.
After they close bedroom door behind them, there
is sudden clatter and confusion as everybody gets
up and leaves table)

DOLORES: I'm leaving too. My hat, my coat—where are
they? (Gets her clothes) I'm leaving. Our job here
is done.

HENRY: Where are you going?

DOLORES: Where I came from. Back to the city. And you?
You—going too?

HENRY: Yes.

MALCHEN: And how do you think you will get back
tonight? It's dark outside.

HENRY: (Shrugs) Just as I came, I guess. I'll take
my chances—

MALCHEN: In this weather? With no warm coat? You're out
of your mind. (Pause) Tell you what. I'll take you
in my car. Here are the keys. It's parked right
outside. Start it for me and warm it up, will you?
I'll just finish cleaning up, then I'll be right with
you, and we can go—

KARL: Hold it. Just a minute. Do you know what you
are doing?

MALCHEN: Just doing what's natural. Cars are for driving,
right? Mine is old, but in good shape. Winter tires,

too. So (To Henry) here's the key. Just start the car
for me. (There's some hustle and bustle as Dolores
and Henry get ready. Henry is uncertain, shakes
his head, but finally leaves after Dolores takes him
by the arm and pushes him through front door.
Wind noises, snow, etc. As they are leaving, the
light curtain comes down separating front from
backstage. On front stage left, crowing around
artificial fire, sit Lucifer, Samiel, Uriel. There are
receding shouts of 'thank you,' good-bye', etc. Car
doors slam. Engine turns over, eventually starts)

KARL: (Helps Malchen putting chairs back in place, etc.)
Well, our visitors are gone. Did you know what
you were doing? You think they will really wait
for you ? Or drive off without you?

MALCHEN: I believe they'll wait. Besides, I'm almost
finished here, and I'll be right out with them.
Where's my coat—

KARL: (Has put on his coat, sits down) You always
believe, don't you? Believe in—people—

MALCHEN: (Putting on her coat) You're a fine one to
complain about _that_. Yes—I always believe.
Always have—

LUCIFER: (To S/U) Better listen carefully, you guys. We
might learn something. (Pause) Unless you want
to continue picking up wood. (Pause) And write
down what she says, Uriel.

SAMIEL: I brought the tape recorder, boss. Want me to use

it? Now? (Pulls tape recorder from under his coat.
Fluorescent surface. Rewinds it, eerie space noises)
MALCHEN: What's that? What is this noise? (She goes
around the room cleaning and tidying up)
KARL: Just the wind, I guess. Just the wind outside. (Car
horn sounds) You're right. I shouldn't criticize
you. Myself—I do more than just believe. I try, at
least—I give people work in the plant. Housing,
too, and wood in winter—-
MALCHEN: And sometimes in the summer corn and
potatoes, too. I've seen you do it. I remember.
What I didn't know was that you're the boss—
SAMIEL: Hear that, boss? Corn and tomatoes.
URIEL: Yeah—hear that. Sounds better than picking
up wood.
SAMIEL: Oh, shut up, Uriel. Listen and learn. (Both move
closer to curtain. Lucifer follows)
MALCHEN: I—I seem to be hearing things—like voices—
KARL: Probably the two out in the car. Never mind.
(Pause) You are right.Wood in winter and
vegetables in summer. I like to keep a big garden.
(Pause) And some of the workers have stayed on
for years in my plant. Your husband did.
MALCHEN: Always the idealist, aren't you.
KARL: I did enough crazy things in my youth. Didn't
bring me much happiness. Now I try something
different—-
MALCHEN: (Opens window) Let's hear if the car is still

warming. (Listens Distant car noises) You see.
They're still there. (Pause. She shuts window.
Myself—I look at it differently.

LUCIFER: The car. The car. Uriel—get to the car. Get after
the boy—

URIEL: Send Sam, boss. He's stronger. Besides, I want to
hear what she's saying. Maybe we can learn
something new. (To Samiel) Sam—you go to the
car. And give me the tape recorder. (S/U scuffle)

LUCIFER: (Very angry) Oh-damn both of you. Damn and
double damn. You stay here and cool your four
letters—I'll do the job myself— (Storms off, but only
to edge of stage where he stops and listens)

MALCHEN: (Who has meanwhile gotten dressed) I have a
different theory—

KARL: (Joins her at the door where both check locks, etc.)
How—different?

MALCHEN: It's not the _doing_ that matters, but the _spirit_ of
doing. The spirit—

URIEL: (Runs after Lucifer, brings him back on stage) Get
back here, boss. She's talking about _us_.

MALCHEN: When you do something right, and have the
right spirit with it—or when you just think right
thoughts—think and hope—you create some
thing, some kind of energy—spirit energy. (Pause.
She walks back into room) All around us there's
this—this energy which we can create, to which
we can add or from which we can borrow,

anywhere, any time—And somewhere, miles
away— (She and Karl walk through front door,
around curtain to front part of stage keeping to the
other side than that occupied by L/S/U)

LUCIFER: You get this, boys. Play this part back, Sam. It's
important. (Sam does as told, playback noises)

MALCHEN: (To Karl, from front part of stage) Far away, or
maybe nearby, there's somebody who might
borrow from that energy bank. Might want to use
some, for something that has to be done.
Something right but hard—(Animated) Take that
boy, Henry. You heard him tell his story, just a
little while ago. Where did he get the energy to
walk here, all alone, through snow and storm?
(Pause) But—enough of these dreams. Enough
philosophy. Better go to the car now. You
coming, too?

KARL: If you want me to, yes—

MALCHEN: If you wouldn't mind. (Pause) There wasn't
much gas left in the car—just enough to get us to
the station, near your plant—you know. If he's
closed up already, maybe he'd open up just
for you—

KARL: Yes, he would. He's a good friend.

MALCHEN: Also, we might meet Mike on the way to the
city. And offer him a lift. And he might still be in
a foul mood—

KARL: At least, I took his knife—

LUCIFER: Clever dame, that one. Thinks of just about every angle. (Pause) Interesting idea she has, too. Let's get to work on her. Let's adapt. What's good for one shoe is good enough for the other. (Playacts) Spirit energy—write that down, Uriel. And you, Sam, take good care of the tape—The idea—spirit energy—created and deposited in a kind of bank—the idea. Let's check it out, boys, right?

S/U: Right, boss. Why not? What the hell—(They put out their lamps and lighters, then walk off stage left. Karl and Malchen have briefly returned to cottage to turn off light in living room. Now they reappear stage right)

MALCHEN: Didn't you forget something else? You promised them presents in your letter. Gifts. (Laughs) Remember?

KARL: Yes, I do. (Pause) Dolores Messenger, she got her money, her 500—

MALCHEN: But—that was _before_ —before she came here.

KARL: I know (Pause. While they are talking there are intermittent car noises, horn, wind, etc. Slowly on stage left, the throne reappears, pushed by S/U, with Lucifer sitting and writing. All in darkness)

MALCHEN: And the other two—Mike and the young man, Henry. How about them?

KARL: (Laugh) Offends your sense of justice, right?

MALCHEN: It does. Especially when something is put in writing.

KARL: Well—the other two got their gifts, too.

MALCHEN: How?

KARL: *Their* present was—their giving. (Slow and clear)
        The giving was their gift. You understand?

KARL: What's so funny then? I didn't mean it to be a joke.
        Are you laughing about me? About my dreams?
        (Begins to laugh, too) You're right. They sound
        like fairy tales, child's dreams—

MALCHEN: (While she talks, Lucifer, holding tape recorder,
        moves closer to her) No, no—it isn't that. It isn't
        that at all. It's the way you said 'gift' — 'gift'.
        That's what's so funny. (Laugh)

KARL: Well, I'm glad somebody is amused. The three
        visitors didn't find anything funny in all this—

MALCHEN: But it is funny. (Takes Karl's arm) You see—in
        our house, when I was a little girl—my grand-
        mother—she was the first to call me 'Malchen'—
        heaven knows why—she was born and raised in
        Germany. And she always told us children at
        Christmastime—(Imitates accent) 'And at
        Christmas' —that's the way she used to talk— 'at
        Christmas I want no gift, children. You hear me—
        no gift.'

KARL: Why:

MALCHEN: That's just what we used to ask her—why? Why
        no gift? At Christmas? And finally, one year, she
        told us—(Accent) 'Because in German— "gift"
        means "poison"—that's why I want no gift at

Christmas.' (Laughter. Samiel begins to laugh, too,
but is silenced by kick from Uriel. Then Lucifer
begins to laugh, and all five laugh for a
short while)

Karl: No gift for Christmas, huh? Well—that would just
about kill my theories, wouldn't it? (Laugh, then
serious) My father's folks came from eastern
Europe. And I remember, they exchanged gifts in
early January, on Three Kings Day. In January,
couple of weeks from now. And our whole family
used to get together for a second Christmas—and
some of the cousins used to dress up. The Three
Kings. And acted out a little play about them.
(Pause) How beautiful it all was. How well I
remember. As if it was today—
(Car horn, several times)

MALCHEN: Now—let's not start dreaming again. Let's go,
or they'll really leave without us. (Both go off
quickly, stage right)

Lucifer: (From throne, not lit) Hold it, hold it, Karl. (Opens
ledger) Just a minute. Why are you talking about
January, already? Haven't you forgotten something? There's another feast, first. Another cel-e-
bra-tion. New Year? Did you forget New Year?
(He gets off his chair, steps behind throne, takes
key and opens up the doors covering mirror)
Myself— (Grandly) I never forget. Never. (He
strips off his black suit and is now dressed in a

white, tight-fitting suit that under changing lights gradually turns red. He puts on various items that make him look more and more like 'Baby New Year') There—Hear I am. Ready. New Year. (Pause, appropriate music) Ready? Or—did I forget something, too? (Pause. In the following final scene lots of appropriate playacting, sometimes ad-lib) I did—I forgot the key. The key. The boy— young man, rather—bless him. (Pause) He was— the key. Now—a key can turn one way or the other. For opening or closing. (Demonstrates on mirror doors) Either way, it's necessary. And useful, most useful. (Demonstrates again) And so it was with Henry. If our plan had worked out—there would have been no gold. No gold for the baby. (Closes mirror doors sharply) Pity. (Noises of starting car) So—we turn the key the other way. Lock up, and think of something else. New Year. Work harder in the New Year. That's always a good res-o-lu-tion—right? (Very loud, with echo) Harder—work harder. (He goes back to his chair, strikes bell several times, snaps his fingers. Suddenly there appear a number of S/U's, all dressed alike. They pick up (or pull) throne. Lucifer reaches under his chair, takes out bull whip, or similar appropriate item, which he uses abundantly while he and his throne are carried or pulled off. Shouts, noise, music, etc.)— The End.

⚔ THE GUEST ⚔

A Serio-Comedy

THE CAST:

Sam Hershey, attorney and politician

Claudia Hershey, his wife

Brian Hershey, John Hershey, their children, students

Fred Smith, friend of the Hersheys, an investor

Richard Brown, an idealist

Roberta, a maid

Servant

Policeman

Celia, Sam's Mother

⋈ ACT I, SCENE 1 ⋈

The Hersheys' living room. Affluent suburbia. Tasteful decor and furnishing. Piano. Front door, side door to kitchen, back door. Short pause after curtain rises, then enter Claudia with flowers

CLAUDIA: And the roses? Right there, on the piano, so that he will see them right away when he comes in. (Places flowers) Perhaps he'll even notice that they are especially for him. We had them delivered this morning. Could have picked some of our own but their stems aren't long enough yet. Or perhaps here, on the table? After all, flowers on the piano doesn't exactly speak of culture. (Switches flowers, stumbles) Damn! The choices one has in life! The decisions one has to make. I wish Sam were here to help me instead of playing golf. But then, he would only argue. Argue and criticize. (Mimics) 'Don't we have enough flowers already?' Criticize and become suspicious. But let him. It's part of profession. How else would he win his court cases? Enough of that. Too much thinking is of no use, especially in the morning. It's like——mental drinking , one could say. (Sits down) Of no use and tiring besides. And the party isn't until this afternoon. And it's HIS party!

(Loud noises offstage, mixed with persistent knocking)

VOICE: (Celia's) Claudia! Claudia!

CLAUDIA: Yes, Mother.

CELIA: I'm ready now. Just finished combing my hair. So you can bring me breakfast now.

CLAUDIA: (Aside) Oh—go and fix your own breakfast. You're perfectly able to do it. (Loud) Yes, Mother. Right away. (Aside) Or hire a housekeeper. You've got the money. (Loud) Eggs again today?

CELIA: Yes, two. And hard-boiled. Good and hard. Yesterday's were too soft.

CLAUDIA: (Aside) Good and hard like yourself. And I did them five minutes yesterday. (Loud) Yes, Mother. Two eggs, hard-boiled. That will take five minutes. (Enter Brian Hershey, a college student. Careless dress and demeanor)

BRIAN: Morning, Mom. Why all the shouting and knocking? It's Saturday. I would have slept longer.

CLAUDIA: And good morning to you too, Brian. But don't complain to me about it. It's your grandmother who started it all.

BRIAN: I know, I know. The usual scene. Breakfast. Two eggs. I heard some of your conversation.

CLAUDIA: And hard-boiled. Extra hard, yet! (She takes flowers back to piano)

BRIAN: Well, I'll just have to start practicing earlier than usual. (Walks to piano) Look at all these flowers. What are they for anyhow?

CLAUDIA: Just getting ready for the party. Remember? This afternoon, for Fred?

BRIAN: Fred?

CLAUDIA Yes, Fred. Your Uncle Fred. (She has put flowers back on piano, then leaves by back door. Brian takes flowers off piano and places them on table. Sits down on piano bench and starts practicing scales. More knocking)

⚜ Act I, Scene 2 ⚜

CLAUDIA: (Returns by back door, now wearing
kitchen apron. Tries whistling along with Brian's
playing) So, that's done now except for the eggs.
They'll take a few more minutes. I'll set the
buzzer. (Goes to desk and sits down) Brian, I wish
you'd play something besides those scales.
Something happy, maybe? (Brian turns head in
her direction but doesn't stop playing. Same scales
but more softly)

BRIAN: That better?

CLAUDIA: The volume—yes. The scales—no. And remember
when your father comes home—he doesn't want
to hear any music in the living room. Especially
not on Saturday morning, after his golf game.

BRIAN: I know. (Stops playing) But who is that Uncle
Fred, really? Not Father's brother, is he?
His cousin?

CLAUDIA: (Again moving flowers around. Puts arms
around the bouquet she had just brought in)
Damn!

BRIAN: What's the matter?

CLAUDIA: Damn pricks!

BRIAN: That's what you get for trying to hug a bunch of

roses! Almost like kissing a snake!

CLAUDIA: Some people do it!

BRIAN: And get bitten.

CLAUDIA: And stung. (Goes back to desk. Brian resumes his
playing) Now what else is there this afternoon?
(Looks at desk calendar) Oh yes, call Roberta.
Remind her to come around three so that she can
help me with those last minute preparations.
(Whistles or hums. Reaches for phone)

BRIAN: And who's Roberta? (Claudia pushes telephone
buttons. At this moment enter Sam. Middle-aged.
Dressed in fashionable sports clothes.

SAM: Good morning, all! (Looks in direction of piano.
Shakes his head. Walks unsteadily)

CLAUDIA: Good morning, Sam. And how did that meeting
go this morning? Unusual for Saturday, no?

SAM: The meeting was okay. Politics. Lots of words. But
at least we agreed on the next county chairman.
You're looking at him right now!

CLAUDIA: And the golf?

SAM: As usual. High eighties or so. But that doesn't
matter. It's just a game itself. Après-golf! Is there
such an expression? (Walks slowly to Claudia's
desk) I wish—I wish Brian would do his
practicing some other time. And some other place.
At the club, after the game, the winners always try
to encourage the losers. 'You need more practice,
Sam. Practice makes perfect, Sam.' Old chestnuts.

I don't see much perfection in his piano playing.
Not in my position as a listener, as the
innocent victim.

CLAUDIA: (Sharply) Brian! (Louder) Brian! Please
remember what I just told you!
(Music suddenly stops)

BRIAN: All right, Mom. I heard you. (Gets off piano bench.
Takes from behind piano a practice keyboard
which he places on the real one. Continues
'playing') Now—are you satisfied? Music without
sound! Like words without meaning! Ablakura
menapuccy kaclabora! (Practices silently but with
much gusto. Keeps mumbling)

CLAUDIA: O my god—see what you made me do?
(Jumps up)

BRIAN: Who? God?

CLAUDIA: The eggs! (Turning to Sam) YOUR mother's
eggs. Her breakfast. Hard-boiled. And I didn't set
the buzzer! (Rushes out backstage door)

SAM: (Walks and speaks unsteadily) I see the ladies of
the house are again engaging. In battle. (To Brian)
Your mother had better watch out. Two eggs,
hard-boiled. In my mother's hands. Like bullets.
Could mean war! (Slaps Brian on shoulder) Music
without sound, huh? And from you? From one of
your generation? Why—the other day at the club
they had what they called a band. Three players
and thirty pieces of electronic equipment. The

tables were shaking. The bar was shaking. The glasses in our hands were shaking.

(Demonstrates)

BRIAN: (Unruffled) We are told that Beethoven, one of the greatest musicians of all times was deaf at the end of his life. So—some of his beautiful music was to him without sound. Except in his mind, his heart, his soul.

SAM: Is that so? Sitting in the bar that day I almost became deaf myself. Still, there were some people my age who didn't seem to mind the noise at all. They looked almost—ecstatic. Acted ecstatic too!

(Demonstrates)

BRIAN: Dad—-who is Uncle Fred?

SAM: Uncle Fred? Why—-didn't your mother tell you? Ask her! (Claudia returns with plates)

CLAUDIA: Ask me what?

BRIAN: Who is Uncle Fred? What relation is he to us? Your cousin? Dad's?

CLAUDIA: You and your questions. Every since you were a baby! Ever since you could talk—questions, questions. Other kids your age got into trouble taking some of the neighbor's peaches. Or breaking a window with a baseball. You—you asked questions.—-Here, take this plate up to your grandmother. She's been waiting long enough for her eggs. And heaven knows they'll be as hard as pebbles. (Hands plate to Brian. Aside)

Either to sharpen her teeth even more or perhaps
break what's left of them. (Brian exit side door)

SAM: What did you just say?

CLAUDIA: (Back to arranging flowers) What? To Brian?
About the eggs? The hard-boiled eggs?

SAM: No. To yourself.

CLAUDIA: Am I going to be questioned now after all the
work I did? Is this a courtroom or a living room?
Can't you ever leave some of your professional
manners behind in the office?

SAM: And just bring the paycheck home? Sorry,
Claudia. Love me, love my manners.

CLAUDIA: Love? Manners? Airs would be a better word.

SAM: (Loud) Airs? Did you say 'airs'? Haha! That's
good! That's rich! Me and my airs! Sam Hershey's
airs! Sam Hershey's sons! Sam Hershey's tunes!
(Puckers his lips as if to whistle. No sound. Goes
to silent keyboard. Tries playing. No sound) Love
me, love my airs, love my silent tunes!

CLAUDIA: (Has taken vase filled with flowers, presses vase
to herself) Twisting words around. As usual. I said
'airs' would be a better word than 'manners.' I
didn't mean 'airs' like 'tunes.' Or even 'sons.' And
I wasn't talking about love, not I.

SAM: Okay. If you want to argue. Love me, love my
words. How do you think we lawyers make our
living? Mainly with words. Oral or written
words. We use them, interpret them...

CLAUDIA: Twisting them around, maybe? (Defiant. Still
clutching vase of flowers) And why must you
always bring up love? Love me this, love me that?
(Brian returns quietly. Resumes his silent practicing)

SAM: (Sits down facing Claudia) Do we have to go
through that again?

CLAUDIA: That? What? Be specific, for once!

SAM: 'Love me this, love me that'...That I know nothing
about love. That I married you mainly because
your name ends in ...ia——Claudia, like my
mother's——Celia...(Waves arms around)

CLAUDIA: (Very loud) Oh, stop it already! You and your
paranoia! The arguments you always provoke.
Silly and useless. And in front of the children! If any
body could hear you now! (Brian has stopped his
silent practicing and clapped his hands over his
ears. Enter Celia through side door. She walks on
a cane, stiffly but fully alert, hard of hearing)

CELIA: (Loud) This is impossible! Listen to me! (Knocks
cane on floor) No, not
impossible....imp....imp....impalatable...

SAM: Oh, sorry, Mother. I didn't notice you right away.
Good morning to you. Here, have a seat. Sit down
next to me.

CELIA: Thank you, Sam. Somebody at least pays attention
to me. But the noise you can make on a Saturday
morning. Take it easy, like everybody else. And
what was I saying just saying?

SAM: Some word with 'imp....'

CELIA: Im...pal...at...able.

SAM: Inedible

CELIA: In..del...ible? I wouldn't know anything about
          that. You are the word master around here. The
          simple fact is: I couldn't eat them!

SAM: What? The words?

CELIA: (Sharply) The eggs. The words... you must eat
          them yourself often enough.

CLAUDIA: You wanted them hard-boiled. You said so,
          specifically. And now you complain.

SAM: (Gets up) The question here is: what exactly is
          hard-boiled? Hard as what? Old cheese? Hard
          rubber? A rock? Interpretation, that is the root of
          the question. Interpretation and definition.
          (Goes to bar, pours drink)

BRIAN: (Takes silent keyboard off piano, then slams both
          hands on the real keyboard a few times. Brief
          silence) Questions? You are so right, Mother. And
          my question is: who's Uncle Fred? And nobody
          will answer me. Grandmother, will you? Will you
          tell me who is Uncle Fred? Mother is making so
          much of his visit. Flowers everywhere. Special
          help in the afternoon. Caterers even, maybe.
          And Dad just shakes his head and tells me to ask
          Mom. Well?

CELIA: First answer my question, Brian. Can I eat this
          hard-boiled egg without...

CLAUDIA: Oh, stop it, will you. I heard you the first time. I'm sorry the eggs got overdone and I'll try to do better next time. Exasperating...how in a home like ours a small mistake can become a big problem. Just because some people don't stop fretting or talking about it. (To Brian) As to your question, Brian, Why don't you go and ask him yourself?

BRIAN: Myself? Go and ask Uncle Fred who he is?

CLAUDIA: That's what I meant. A young man like yourself...if you can't get the right answer at home, go and look for it outside. Fred is staying at the Midtown Plaza Hotel. So...

BRIAN: Okay, if that's what you think I should do. It's logical. If you cannot find the answer inside, look for it outside, and vice versa. Can I have the car keys?

SAM: Not mine! Ride your bicycle or take the bus, or whatever...

BRIAN: To the Midtown Plaza? There might be a bus in an hour or so. Bicycle would take at least that long. Anyhow, I thought Uncle Fred was coming here this afternoon. So...

CLAUDIA: Here, take my keys, Brian. Drive carefully. Remind Fred we'll expect him in the early afternoon. He's a little forgetful sometimes... (Throws car keys to him. Brian gets up from piano bench)

SAM: (Drink in hand. Unsteady voice) Just a second, Brian. Didn't I just say...

BRIAN: I heard you say 'whatever.' So that would include Mom's car, right? Thanks, Mom. Don't worry, Dad. I'll be careful. So long, everybody! See you all later! (Exit. Moment of silence)

SAM: (Sharply to Claudia) Now why did you do that?

CLAUDIA: What?

SAM: Give Brian your car keys.

CLAUDIA: Because.

SAM: Because what?

CLAUDIA: Because he asked for them.

SAM: To go downtown? To see Fred? Uncle Fred? Your friend Fred?

CLAUDIA: Stop it right there, Mister Attorney. Whose friend? Mine? No so! Yours! Your friend, right? Your school friend, right?

SAM: Right.

CLAUDIA: And wasn't it you yourself who introduced him to me?

SAM: Yes. At a party. Some time ago. I hadn't seen Fred for years, many years. And suddenly there he was, at this party. Our class reunion, in fact. Cut quite a figure, Fred, and the word soon spread that he had been very successful in life. I could believe it. He'd always had many interests. In school there wasn't a subject he disliked or wasn't at least good at...

CLAUDIA: So?

SAM: So? So when he sat down at the piano that after

noon, in the club...

CLAUDIA: I remember, yes...

SAM: I didn't ask you to sit down next to him on the bench and start banging away...

CLAUDIA: You didn't have to ask me, Sam. I did it quite on my own. Spontaneously.

SAM: Now who has the big words? Just listen to her...In any case, it caused quite a stir...

CLAUDIA: Did we? I am glad. As for 'banging away', as you put it, we didn't. We played quite well. Maybe we'll do it again this afternoon. Except that I'm out of practice...

SAM: At playing? You can say that again!

CELIA: (Banging her cane several times) Stop arguing! Both of you. Remember, Sam, this is your home, not a courtroom.

CLAUDIA: Just what I have been trying to tell him.

SAM: Just because you don't like to argue. You're not good at it! Always changing in midstream.

CLAUDIA: Changing what?

SAM: Topics.

CLAUDIA: Shouldn't it be horses?

SAM: Topics—horses—-tops, for all I care. (Pause, then to Celia who has been tossing eggs in the air, off and on, during this scene) And what are you doing, Mother? Planning to join the circus?

CELIA: Thank you, Sam. Don't have to. Already am a member of one. I'm just doing this for my—my—

re-flex-es. Also I hear movement is good for my arthritis. So you see the hard-boiled eggs are good for something after all.

CLAUDIA: But you did eat one of them, right?

CELIA: Eat it? Swallow it whole is more like it. Now it's lying down there in my stomach like a boat sunk to the bottom of the ocean. (Gets up slowly)

CLAUDIA: How poetic you can be, Mother. Your language— it's almost—romantic.

CELIA: Whatever romance is there in an egg tossing around undigested in one's stomach? But in any case, watch yourself this afternoon, you hear!

SAM: Who, me? You mean with Fred. Arm in arm maybe? That would be a sight.

CLAUDIA: She means me, probably. Still I don't know what there would be to watch or watch out for. Because of what Sam said about our little piano playing? Ridiculous!

SAM: I don't know. I don't have the right words for it. But I have that feeling.

CLAUDIA: (Laughing out loud) You? You don't have the right words? And instead feelings? I bet you'd never get away with that in court.

SAM: Get away with what? Be precise!

CLAUDIA: (Imitating him) Be precise! All right then. You'd never get away with running out of words and showing feelings instead.

SAM: (Seriously) It would be difficult. But believe it or

not, many times we rely on our feelings. Especially when we appraise people, clients or opponents. And often feelings are proven to be right even though they cannot be substitutes for reason and words when it comes to winning a case.

CLAUDIA: (Steps forward) Well, this time you're not going to win a case because there is no case to win. (To Celia) I'll take these eggs away now. I said I was sorry they overcooked. I'll do better tomorrow. As for today, the party this afternoon—-don't worry, Sam. Fred is your school friend. And I'll behave myself. (Tosses egg in the air) Let me just call Roberta again and make sure she'll be here in time to help me. (Exit to kitchen)

SAM: (Sits down on Sofa next to Celia. Drinks) How hard it is to argue with someone who's always right. Or at least thinks so.

CELIA: She's your wife. You ought to have trained her differently.

SAM: Trained her? She's no animal. And this is a home, not a circus. Besides, it was you who said I should marry her, remember?

CELIA: Because her name ends in—-ia, like my own. And Claudia is such a nice name, so class—i—cal and no—ble.

SAM: Like Celia...

CELIA: No. Celia is just an ab—bre—vi—a—tion. But it will do!

SAM: An abbreviation? Well now, that's one thing my
         mother will never be, an abbreviation. The whole
         thing, yes! The complete item! No less. But here's
         Claudia. (To Claudia who has entered through
         kitchen door) Did you know that your name is...

CELIA: (Knocks cane on floor) Stop it!

CLAUDIA: Still couldn't reach Roberta. I also checked with
         the agency Roberta works for. This is the number
         of the party she's working for this morning. I
         guess I'd better start with the final touches myself...

SAM: Final touches? Is that what you said?

CLAUDIA: Yes. (Starts dusting) Anything wrong with that?

SAM: No, nothing at all. Just that I haven't seen you so
         interested in housework for some time. But then—
         nothing's too much work for Uncle Fred, right?

CLAUDIA: (Stops work for a moment) Sounds like
         you're jealous.

SAM: Jealousy is...is like a sickness caused by the virus
         of disillusionment.

CLAUDIA: (Back to dusting. Sneezes) Yes, Doctor, and
         you're immune. I suppose. For a time anyhow.

SAM: And what's that supposed to mean?

CLAUDIA: Oh, nothing.

SAM: Then why say it? To have the last word, I suppose.
         (Drinks) Oh, what's the use! At work, arguing
         earns me money and respect. At home the money
         is spent and arguing earns me nothing, respect
         least of all. There is another bizarre case for you.

CLAUDIA: For me? Another? You mean something bizarre is already happening?

SAM: For you—collectively meaning, for everybody. Can't you see anything my way today? Is your mind not working on Saturdays? Or are you so mixed up and nervous? (Grandly) Just another case, I said. A case of taking and giving. Like inhaling and exhaling. Here—(Demonstrates)

CLAUDIA: My word! All that hot air! Soon the whole house will rise like a balloon and all of us with it in the gondola...(Demonstrates)

CELIA: Not me! I'm staying right here. (Gets up) Now, quiet you two! I hear somebody coming in.

CLAUDIA: Probably 'No-No', I mean—John. He did some last minute shopping for me. (Enter through front door John Hershey, sometimes called 'No-No' at home, carrying grocery bags. High school student. Clean dress and looks. As soon as he enters Sam puts drink down and Claudia her dust cloth. Both sit down)

JOHN: Hi, everybody. (Pause) And how is everybody? Family council? The quiet after a storm? Or perhaps before one? I bought your groceries, Mom. Anything else I can do for you?

CLAUDIA:No, No-No! Thank you. Just take the groceries into the kitchen for me, please. (Exit John. Sam and Claudia get up)

SAM: No-No? I thought we all agreed some time ago

that John should be be plain John as soon as he
becomes a senior. He's a senior now, so——

CLAUDIA: Senior? That sounds old to me. To me he's still
our youngest and my baby.

SAM: To you, maybe. Not to me. Baby? Are you crazy?
Time you grow up yourself and act your age!
(Reenter John. Sam and Claudia sit down. Pause)

CLAUDIA: So there you are, No——, excuse me——John.
Thank you again for your help. And don't forget
this afternoon. Your Uncle Fred is coming. His
birthday is sometime this month and we want to
surprise him. You remember your Uncle Fred,
don't you?

JOHN: Of course I do. Especially the three weeks Brian
and I spent with him. When was it? Four years
ago? Five?

CLAUDIA: Just four, dear. Four years ago.

JOHN: (Slowly, as if in a dream) I don't remember ever
having been so happy in my life. Before our visit
and since.

CLAUDIA: That's a strange thing to say. You don't seem
exactly unhappy here, in your own home. Unless
you're putting on an awfully good act.

JOHN: I don't mean it that way.

CLAUDIA: Well, how do you mean it then? Tell us, please.

JOHN: I mean that those three weeks were different. It
was kind of peaceful there at his ranch out west.
That uncle——whatever kind of uncle he may be, I

don't really care—he had things for us to do each each day. He let us drive his tractor and even his pickup. Or we went to visit places like museums or amusement parks. That was it! We did things together. Life was—was balanced in a way. Balanced and relaxing.

SAM: Not like here, huh? In your home, right?

JOHN: Home is different. Home is life. And life is more— I don't really know how to put it—life is more tension than relaxation, I guess.

CLAUDIA: (After a pause) Just listen to him. Our youngest, our No-No, our baby...

SAM: I heard it. Quite a speech. Seems we have a philosopher in the house.

JOHN: Whatever...I had better change now and be off...

CLAUDIA: Why? Aren't you going to stay for the party?

JOHN: I'm going to the club and play tennis for a while. We have a special kind of matches planned for today. But I'll be back in time for Uncle Fred's party. (Leaves through front door)

CLAUDIA: This boy never fails to surprise. This baby of mine, this No-(Puts hand over her mouth) The ideas he has and the way he describes them! Amazing!

SAM: I agree. He might make a good lawyer one day. But right now, I think we should no longer call 'No-No'. He's really too old for that.

CLAUDIA: Too old? Perhaps. His classmates gave him that

name back in second or third grade, I think.

SAM: Because he said 'no-no' so often in school, almost like a record. Said it just the way you said it to him at home. Slightest thing he'd do wrong and off you went: 'No, no, Johnnie. Don't do that! No, no.'

CLAUDIA: So, it's all my fault again, is it? Only this time there is no truth in what you're saying, none at all.

SAM: I'm only relating what Brian told me. I'm trying to explain it his way. Brian, your oldest, always could do as he pleased. But for John it was always 'no, no.' That's how Brian put it: 'Mom was always no-noing John...'

CLAUDIA: (Shrieks) Oh no, no-no (John has entered through the side door. He is dressed like a hobo)

SAM: (Jumps up) Hey! What the Sam Hill! What's going on here?

CLAUDIA: (Covers face with her hands) Is that really you, John? Now I've seen it all! No, it can't be! No, no...

JOHN: Surprised, aren't you! I'd be too. Hobos are a rare sight in this clean and clear-cut world of ours. I read that there was a time when railroad tracks ran through our town, along Main Street, I believe. And with the railroad came hobos, as they were called. People, mostly men, who rode the trains for free, like the birds that squat on our trees without paying rent. Adventure drove them on or perhaps restlessness. Or they simply wanted to live differently.

SAM: And now you want to be one too? A hobo? No, no, that will never do! Not my son! No, sir!

JOHN: Just for a little while, Dad. Just for a couple of hours (Sits down) You see, I thought we'd have a party. In the club. A hobo party.

CLAUDIA: You mean something like Halloween? Aren't you and your friends a little too old for that?

JOHN: (Enthusiastically) It's only for the tennis players. Everybody comes dressed like a hobo or clown. And one of the conditions is long pants. Everybody must also wear long pants.

CLAUDIA: Why?

JOHN: So the odds of winning a set are perhaps a little better for the poorer players.

CLAUDIA: I don't see the point, dear.

JOHN: Well, in long pants and baggy clothes no player will be as fast as usual.

(Gets up and demonstrates)

SAM: Sounds interesting but won't work.

JOHN: Why not?

SAM: Because your better players will always be better, even if they wear long pants. And the best will always be the best. That's life, John, that's life. And that's why we no longer have hobos in our town.

JOHN: Yes. But there's still another condition all the players have agreed to.

SAM Well?

JOHN: I'll tell you after I come back. After I've found out if it has worked.

CELIA: (Struggles to get up and finally does. Swings her cane like a tennis rack) How about me? I can wear pants too. So can I come along?

JOHN: Not today, Grandma. Some day we must have a special party for all the grandparents.

SAM: The imagination this boy has! Whose ideas are these, anyhow?

JOHN: (Loud) They are your son's, Dad. They are your son's ideas. So long, everybody. See you in a few hours.

SAM: My son's ideas? Will I ever catch up with his thoughts? His plans? His lifestyle? Will any father, ever? (Runs toward front door) Wait, John, wait for me. (Finishes drink) Be careful when you jump on that train! And save a seat for me!

CELIA: And me!

(Both exit front door after John. End of Act I)

⊰ ACT II ⊱

A suite in an exclusive hotel. Elegant furnishings. Full living room and part of a bedroom. As curtain opens Fred Smith is pacing the floor. Elegant but somewhat careless dress. Worldly manners. He is holding a cordless phone to his ear. In the bedroom Robbie, the maid, can be seen dusting.

SMITH: (Pushes buttons then talks) Fred Smith here. Yes, you heard correctly. Fred Smith, no more, no less. Where are we right now with Actium Industries? 150? That's good, right? No, don't sell, not yet. It's going to go higher. Yes, I know. We waited all morning yesterday. But with 10,000 shares it's worth it. What did you say? Movement? In Hong Kong? Down or up? Not sure? Well, find out. Yes, I'll hold. (While keeping the phone to his ear Fred Smith does some dance steps then speaks to audience) How convenient and pleasant. Music with your business. As if the world were one long song. (Pause) And how polite some people can be on the phone. (Into phone) What? You cannot find out. What? Weekend? Yes, I know. No, I said, dammit!! No, no! (To audience again) Where was

I? Oh yes, the pleasures of polite business, voice to voice rather than face to face. Excuse my dancing around, but if I don't move this music will put me to sleep. Perhaps that's the real purpose of music? (Another phone rings. Smith reaches into his pocket for another phone) Smith here. Speak louder, please. What? Yes, I know you're shouting! Taiwan? Down to 78? Then sell, for god's sake! (Puts phone back into pocket. To audience) What god, she wants to know. As if it made any difference. As if God had anything to do with this——this kind of business. (Sits on sofa) Will it always be like this? Will the heart always be where the money is? Does it have to be so? (Gets up, pours drink. Enter from bedroom Robbie in maid's dress. Quiet in manner and speech)

ROBBIE: Excuse me, Mr. Smith, but are you off the phone for a minute?

SMITH: (Pulls phone from pocket) Off one, on another. (Listens) Still on music. You see, Robbie, it's—it's an exercise. Like walking forward and back again. (Demonstrates) But go ahead and start your vacuum now. It too makes music of a sort. Not exactly for dancing. But then, you don't expect to dance while you do your cleaning, Robbie? Or do you?

ROBBIE: It's not that, Mr. Smith.
(Takes vacuum cleaner from closet)

Smith: What is it then?

Robbie: Well, Mr. Smith, you see——I was thinking——one day last week you were telling me about—I mean—what you thought about liberty.

Smith: Did I?

Robbie: Yes. You were on the telephone, like today. You said something like you were exercising your freedom. By buying and selling. And what a wonderful life that was. Remember?

Smith: Sometimes I get carried away, I know. Then I dream about things, things like liberty or even love. And then I wake up and remember the——-the fire that comes with both of these. Lady Liberty and her torch...

Robbie: Well, anyhow, Mr. Smith——I took the liberty of leaving this room number at the desk downstairs. So that my agency can call me and confirm the special assignment I took for this afternoon. A party job...

Smith: Special job? This afternoon? You took the liberty? I don't understand. I thought you'd be available all day...

Robbie: We talked about that too last week. You said you'd be at a party this afternoon. So I told the agency I could take on an extra job—for special pay——weekend, you know.

Smith: And we discussed all of this? Well then, if you say so! I hope that job really does pay well.

ROBBIE: Very well, sir. A hundred for three to four hours, just helping out. Plus, I can be back here in the evening.

SMITH: Just helping out, is that it? (Robbie starts vacuum. Smith tries dance steps again but soon gives up. Telephone rings)

ROBBIE: May I take this call, please? Perhaps it will be the agency. (Turns vacuum off, takes phone) Hello? Yes, this is room 314. Yes, ma'am, this is Roberta speaking. Yes, I can come and help out this afternoon. Yes, ma'am, thank you. (Replaces receiver. To Smith) If you don't mind, Mr. Smith, I'll get ready now. And I can finish my work later this evening.

SMITH: Roberta? Did I hear you say Roberta?

ROBBIE: Yes, you did. It's my name for special occasions.

SMITH: Like this afternoon, I suppose. Well, all right then, get ready. I'll have to leave before long, too. (Robbie puts vacuum back into closet. Straightens hair and dress. Exit through bedroom door. Knock on main door) Come in!

SERVANT: A young gentleman to see you, sir. Name's Hershey, Brian Hershey.

SMITH: Brian? Brian Hershey? Yes, of course. Show him in.

BRIAN: (Enters slowly. Looks around a few moments) Hi—Uncle Fred!

SMITH: Hello there. Now this is a surprise. What brings you here? Did your mother send you to make sure

I'll get there on time? A minute late and she gets
furious, right? Or has the party been called off?
Altogether? And she's afraid to tell me?

BRIAN: No, no! None of this, none at all. I just wanted to
talk to you!

SMITH: Talk to me? A private matter? Good idea. (Both sit
down) Party talk is mostly just chatter. Serious
talk is something different. Tell you what—let's
have lunch together. Would that be okay?

BRIAN: I haven't even had breakfast today.

SMITH: Okay then. I'll have food brought up for us. (Rings
bell. Servant enters, waits at door) Could you
bring up lunch for two, please.
Something substantial.

SERVANT: Very well, sir. Lunch for two. Will steaks be all
right? Or chicken on toast?

SMITH: Whatever. You decide, Brian. What do you want?

BRIAN: 'Whatever' sounds good enough for me, too.

SMITH: (To Servant) So, you make the decision. (Servant
bows and exits) (To Brian) That was easy, wasn't it?

BRIAN: It seemed to be. Get somebody else to make your
decisions. (Looks around) I guess that goes with a
life of leisure.

SMITH: Which young people, often find hard to understand, or approve of. But leisure, as you call it, is
not the same as laziness. Leisure constructively
lived, can become the apex of success in life.

BRIAN: I wouldn't know much about that. My studies

give me little time to experiment with leisure, right now.

SMITH: And how are your parents? (Robbie can be seen in bedroom, changing clothes to get ready for her next assignment)

BRIAN: They are okay, thank you.

SMITH: And your brother John? Do they still call him 'No-No'? As they used to?

BRIAN: Mother does, sometimes. I guess she doesn't want to let go. Doesn't want to lose her 'baby', as Dad puts it. They argue about this. Often.

SMITH: Strange name, this 'No-No'. I wonder how he got it.

BRIAN: That's what they argue about. Dad says the name stuck because Mom always said 'no, no' to him. Any time he coughed or sneezed out of turn. Or did anything she didn't expect him to do. It seems she wanted him to be the perfect child...

SMITH: A romantic idea——looking for perfection in a human being.

BRIAN: Well, actually, the real reason John got this strange name——(Knock at door. Enter Servant with food cart. Begins to set table for lunch. Conversation stops for a moment. Robbie can be seen finishing her work in the bedroom)

SMITH: Let's have lunch now. We can continue the conversation at the table. (Both sit down at lunch table. Servant serves food)

BRIAN: John's classmates gave him that strange name——

'No-no'.

SMITH: Oh?

BRIAN Say—you won't tell my brother I told you this
story, will you? He always seems to be a little
embarrassed about it.

SMITH: Tell John? Of course not.

BRIAN: Well—as John himself tells it, it happened some
years back in fourth or fifth grade. John had got
into the habit of taking charge.

SMITH: Of what?

BRIAN: Whatever there was to take charge of. The class
room when the teacher had to leave for a while or
games at the playground.

SMITH: And that explains 'No-No'?

BRIAN: It does. Whenever John took charge his first words
would always be: 'No nonsense now. Let's
get organized!'

SMITH: (Laughs) So, that's it. No-No—no nonsense. I like
that (Muffled ringing of telephone. Smith reaches
into inside coat pocket, takes out phone, listens,
then speaks) No, no, I don't care how low it is.
Speak louder please. No, I said. Don't scream, I
know you're in Hong Kong. But I'm not buying.
(Sharply) Not today. And that's final! (Replaces
phone in coat pocket. Telephone! Brings you your
business wherever you might be sitting.
Convenience? Or modern dependency? Slavery?

BRIAN: Why didn't you buy while the stock is low?

SMITH: Because I didn't want to, that's all.

BRIAN: (After a pause in which they have begun to eat) Tell me, Uncle Fred, what kind of uncle are you, really? How are we related? By Blood? Marriage? Choice? (Another pause. Robbie can be seen leaving by side door)

SMITH: Does it really matter? Isn't much of anybody's personal relationship coincidental? But if you really must know—yes, in fact there is a distant relationship by marriage between you father and myself. Mostly, however, our relationship was established years ago when we attended the same school together.

BRIAN: And that calls for "Uncle" Fred?

SMITH: More by default, so to speak. And of course only by mutual consent.

BRIAN: By default?

SMITH: Yes. With both of your parents not having brothers there is a distinct lack of uncles in your family.

BRIAN: So you step in and fill in the void, in a way.

SMITH: You sound displeased with this arrangement.

BRIAN: Because if the relationship you describe is between you and my dad, I don't see the reason for so much interest on my mother's part.

SMITH: So much interest? How?

BRIAN: As shown by the party this afternoon. Personal interest of this kind that leads to quarrels in our home.

SMITH: I don't see anything wrong with personal interest.

BRIAN: Intimate interest that leads to frustration, to tears...

SMITH: Intimate interest? Why shouldn't people have real personal interest for one another?

BRIAN: My dad doesn't see it in this detached way.

SMITH: He doesn't? And you said there are tears at home sometimes? There is frustration? I wasn't aware of all this until right now.

BRIAN: So now you are aware of it, Mr. Smith. (Gets up) Thank you for the lunch. You certainly have a good life here. So long then. (Walks to front door)

SMITH: One minute, please, Brian. (Gets up)

BRIAN: Yes, Mr. Smith?

SMITH: Could it be that your judgment here is a little extreme? Your words sounded so—so dramatic just now.

BRIAN: (After a pause) Perhaps. But I see the situation as it appears to me, from close up. You take a more distant view. You can see what you want to see, no more. (Pause) Thank you again, Mr. Smith.

SMITH: Until later, then.

BRIAN: Maybe. I really have a lot of studying to do this afternoon. Medicine is a tough field. (Leaves through front door)

SMITH: (Sits down) Bother—youth—the age of exaggeration and inflated judgment. Where feeling are expressed openly, where sentiment and song still prevail, unfettered by reason and common sense. (Gets up and walks, reaches for telephone) And love. Wasn't it love that prompted Brian to speak his mind right now? Love for his parents? (Pause) And is there something like love between his mother and me? She talks about it in some of her letters. (Pause) But what are letters, really? Pieces of paper. Feelings and words put into written, material form. And what if there was love? What of it? Isn't love what everybody in the worlds strives for in the end? What every living creature needs and craves? Isn't love the common denominator, so to speak, of all living beings? I'm sorry about this young man's opinion on this. I've always been very fond of the two, Brian and his brother. His brother—John. I can also imagine what John would say about this situation: 'no, no!' No nonsense. (Strong knock at front door) Yes! Come in!

SERVANT: A gentleman here to see you, sir. A Mr. Brown. Here's his card, sir.

SMITH: Richard Brown? Club representative? Hm— (To Servant) A gentleman, you said?

SERVANT: Yes, sir. At least as far as one can tell...

SMITH: What do you mean?

SERVANT: I don't mean to be disrespectful, sir, but—

SMITH: Well, what is it? Out with it!

SERVANT: The face, sir—

Smith: The face?

Servant: The beard, sir—

Smith: The beard? I don't understand...have to see this
         for myself. Show the man in.

Servant: Yes, Sir. (Exits. Enter Richard Brown, the guest.
         Well dressed, showy beard. Servant reenters
         after him)

Brown: May I come in, Mr. Smith?

Smith: Yes, of course. Please do. Have a seat!

Brown: (Looks around carefully) Thank you, Mr. Smith.
         (Looks at Servant, sits down)

Smith: (To Servant) Thank you, Charles. That will be all.
         Servant removes lunch dishes and exits with cart)
         And now, what can I do for you, Mr. Brown?
         (Looks at business card) Mr. Richard Brown, club
         representative, right?

Brown: You can give me money.

Smith: Money?

Brown: Yes. Anything over twenty will do!

Smith: (Laughs) A hundred perhaps? Would a
         hundred do?

Brown: A hundred would do admirably well, Mr. Smith.
         Would also save me additional visits.

Smith: Well now! A most extraordinary offer, I must say.
         (Begins to use phone but does not complete the
         call) Also, your candor is extraordinary. You come
         right out with what you want, right?

Brown: That's the one aspect of my work that I especially

enjoy. It's like——like a part of youth recaptured, the part we so often lose after growing up. Open and close. (Demonstrates by closing and opening fist) It's like work and rest, like inhaling and exhaling. It's a balance, it's life——

SMITH: So, we have here a philosopher, Mr. Brown. Is that what you do as a club representative, as you call yourself? Sell your wisdom? And want to get paid for it? (Gets up) Well, I must say it again, a most unusual proposition.

BROWN: I'm glad you think so. With some of my customers I don't get this far. At the first hint of thought or philosophy, as you call it, they panic. Sometimes even throw me out. You're different, Mr. Smith. I'm not disappointed in you, so far.

SMITH: (Lightly) Well, let's see now. So far you have delivered perhaps a dollar's worth of wisdom. Unsolicited—which means we deduct 50 percent. Fifty cents of wisdom then. But that won't do, right?

BROWN: Right. Fifty cents won't do. Anything under twenty dollars won't do. I have administrative expenses, you know.

SMITH: (Serious again) And one hundred would save you four additional visits?

BROWN: Me and you, right.

SMITH: (Aside) Might almost be worth it, just to get rid of this creep. (Suddenly sharply to Brown) Okay,

Brown, so where's your gun. Show me!

BROWN: There's no gun. Words are my weapon. Less pain, less messy.

SMITH: And less noisy.

BROWN: Sometimes.

SMITH: And if I don't listen to your words?

BROWN: Then I'll just go quietly and try somewhere else. I usually give my clients five minutes to listen to me. Another five if they also hear what I have to say.

SMITH: Listen, hear, and pay, right?

BROWN: Naturally.

SMITH: All right then. Shoot. (Pause. Then sound of an alarm clock from bedroom. Robbie can be seen getting up from bed. Has changed her clothes)

BROWN: (In sudden panic) What's this...this noise I hear?

SMITH: Scares you, huh? Just an alarm clock going off. So don't worry about it.

BROWN: Alarm clock? At this time of day? Are you sure it's not some sort of security system set off by an unwanted intruder?

SMITH: (Amused) Really worried, aren't you? I thought you were going to tell me about your business. What club are you soliciting money for? Or is it another charity?

BROWN: I will! I will tell you. (Gets up, looks around nervously, especially toward bedroom) Club? What kind of club, you're asking? My own club. Myself, actually.

SMITH: (Impatient) Enough of that. Just give me the name and address of the club. (Gets pad of paper and pencil) And I'll write them down.

BROWN: That won't be necessary. You see——some time ago——how long ago was it? Six months? A year? I decided that my regular work, taking care of investments, wasn't really what I wanted to do in life. I felt that something was missing. Something more personal. Or perhaps greater variety.—— I still don't know how to put it in the right words. (Pause) In any case, one day I decided to try a different kind of life. Radically different. Instead of manipulating money, buying and selling stock, you know all about that——I became a beggar——

SMITH: A beggar? How?

BROWN: I went to see casual acquaintances of mine——my friends I'd rather leave out of this——and simply asked them for money.

SMITH: (Laughing) Anything twenty or up, right? Wasn't that new venture of yours rather difficult, to say the least?

BROWN: Yes, very difficult, especially the first few times. The people I approached were surprised, naturally. Annoyed at times. Some thought I had gone bankrupt and wanted to recover my losses.

SMITH: At twenty dollars a shot? Ridiculous. But tell me—— are you?

BROWN: What?

SMITH: Bankrupt.

BROWN: Far from it.

SMITH: So, what do you want my money for?

BROWN: That's exactly what everybody else wants to know. I want money so that I can share it with others.

SMITH: Then why not use your own?

BROWN: That's would be neither fair nor—-fun, if that's the right word. You see, the money I earn in my regular work comes too easily now.

ROBBIE: (Calls from bedroom) Your bedroom is ready now, sir.

SMITH: (Goes to bedroom door) All right, Robbie. Thank you. Until later then. (Robbie leaves through bedroom door and back door. (To Brown) You were saying that things are too easy for you now?

BROWN: Money comes too easily. Goes just as easily too. Like friends.

SMITH: What was that?

BROWN: I already explained to you that I wanted to do things differently in life. I wanted more variety.

SMITH: Isn't there enough variety in business? In buying and selling? Aren't there enough challenges in that? Isn't that life, too?

BROWN: It is, in a way. But as I said before I wanted to share some of the money I made.

SMITH: Charity, right? There's enough of that

around already.

BROWN: Not my way. The money I planned to share I
wanted to have made more like——the hard way.

SMITH: By begging from strangers?

BROWN: Exactly.

SMITH: And then?

BROWN: Then I live differently for a while. I begin by
changing into old clothes, very old clothes. From
there I proceed to change the inside, change my
mind, my heart. I become a tramp, a street person.
Not only in appearance but also here. (Beats his
chest with fist)

SMITH: You mean you _act_ the part of a street person.

BROWN: Yes, in a way you might call it acting. But then I
also share a kind of life, or at least try to, in a
realistic way. Whatever I can earn by begging on a
given day I spend that same day on food, clothing
or whatever need there is.

SMITH: Spend the money? Right away? Every day?

BROWN: No, not every day. I started out one day a month.
Then, after some time, two days. Sometimes I can
even do it one day a week.

SMITH: You mean you work as an—an undercover bum?

BROWN: I never thought of it that way. But it's never easy.
Begging is hard work, especially if you're not used
to it as a way of life.

SMITH: And if you draw a blank, if for instance right now
I don't want to support your strange venture——

BROWN: Then—-well, it has happened. If I haven't had anything to share, I went hungry that day too.

SMITH: And where? Where are you doing these self-imposed works of charity that you yourself admit you want and need for a variety in life? Where do you start out?

BROWN: Downtown, usually. Sometimes I just walk along Main Street. Sometimes I begin at the Mission. I help out with the work there. I share what I have earned. All of it. I try to talk to the destitute and desperate. Try to communicate, see life from their point of view. Some day perhaps I'll even spend the night there.

SMITH: Risky business, huh? Can be dangerous there, I hear.

BROWN: Can be. People sometimes get beaten up, mugged, knifed—-

SMITH: And you want to risk all that? Isn't that the idea of variety taken a little too far?

BROWN: (Gets up) Perhaps.

SMITH: Well, Mr. Brown, I'll tell you what I'll do. Right now I must get ready to go to a party. Old school friend of mine invited me. Sam Hershey, over in Middlefield, attorney and big wheel in politics. Can't say no to him. You come back and see me tomorrow or whenever it's convenient. Okay?

BROWN: Okay, Mr. Smith. Time is one thing of which there is plenty in this business, although as you said

yourself, there are certain risks. And have a good
time at the party in Middlefield.
(Walks to front door)

SMITH: I will, I will. And good luck to you too!
(Curtain on Act II)

⚔ ACT III, SCENE 1 ⚖

The Hersheys' home. Same decor as in Act I, but added to it party decorations of various kinds. Claudia and Fred Smith sit on sofa in foreground. Robbie, now Roberta, is in and out of the kitchen with trays, etc. Claudia and Smith dressed stylishly.

SMITH: At first I was somewhat taken in by his approach. I mean, the nerve of it all. Like—-the very first thing—-no less than twenty dollars.

CLAUDIA: You like his speech then, am I right? Words can have such enormous power. Not only their choice, the right word, that is, but also their sound. The effect is close to that of music. Isn't that so?

SMITH: Yes, his words had their effect. An educated man. No doubt about that. But then—-

CLAUDIA: Yes, Fred—-

SMITH: It's hard to explain. As I said, his words hit the mark, all right, but it was the way he spoke them that made the real impression on me. His ideas sounded interesting, but can you imagine a man like him dressing up as a tramp and sounding all the while like a—-philosopher? Phony, that's what it is. (Gets up and walks almost into Roberta, but doesn't recognize her) And then, all that make-believe of trying to lead one life at daytime and another life at night. Looking for variety and—finding it.

CLAUDIA: Sounds to me like he manages somehow to live out his dreams. (Puts her arm through his) Or perhaps he's looking for more still. To complete his own life. To fulfill secret ambitions. To understand and be understood. Perhaps he really wants to share. Sharing is a kind of love—

SMITH: (Sits down. Claudia beside him) Oh yes. We've heard all this before, haven't we? Heard it, read it in novels, seen it on stage and screen—that idea of seeking to understand, to share, to help. But what else is all of this if not an extension of our own self into the life of others? An expansion of our ego, so to speak.

CLAUDIA: To share—understand—love—

SMITH: Love has nothing to do with it. That man—what was his name? Brown, right, Richard Brown—he told me himself that he never approaches his friends with his ideas of begging and sharing. I guess they'd see right through him, wouldn't they?

CLAUDIA: Oh Fred, how can you be so cynical? When you talk like that you sound old—old for your age.

SMITH: (Gets up) Just as long as I don't _look_ old. That's the most important thing today—good looks—telegenics. That and money—and then you're king. So, let me sound old and cynical. Who cares?

CLAUDIA: Who cares? About how we sound, you mean? About words? Why, everybody does, silly. You just said a little while ago that the sound of your Mr. Brown's words—-

SMITH: My Mr. Brown? You're teasing me, surely. But seriously now—-I wonder how he found me in the first place. What did his business card say? Club representative? That must be it. He must have seen my name in our club directory.

CLAUDIA: Or else—

SMITH: Or else what?

CLAUDIA: Or else he was attracted by your personality, by your—-magnetism.

SMITH: You're dreaming. Claudia, dreaming—-

CLAUDIA: You're right, Fred. When I am with certain people I dream. That makes being with them so special, makes communicating with them so nice.

SMITH: You have a whole house full of people to communicate with, to make conversation, make love—-

CLAUDIA:Yes, but that isn't the same thing. Of course, we communicate with the boys. We talk to them, listen to their problems. And often we end up trying to tell them what to do. Perhaps too often. Sam and I talk of course. Then we end up arguing, each trying to be right in one form or another. And that's not really communication, is it? (Pause.

Claudia gets up, Smith sits down, Claudia sits next to him) And then there is Sam's mother. All she ever does is knock her cane on the floor or at the wall. Her talk is mostly exclamation points. (She sobs, throws her arms around Smith who kisses her quickly, then pushes her gently away. Claudia gets up. Turns stereo on. Dance music. She pulls Smith up from the sofa. They dance for a while)

SMITH: (After both sit down again, Roberta can now be seen going in and and out of the kitchen. Smith follows her with his eyes) Tell me, Claudia, where is everybody?

CLAUDIA: Gone, for the moment at least. Brian to the library, No-No—-I mean John to the club for tennis. Sam to play another round of golf, his mother to bed for a nap, thank God. But they'll all be back. The boys especially want to see their Uncle Fred. And this is your birthday, right?

SMITH: Well, actually it was last week.

CLAUDIA: Was? Last week? And I forgot? How could I? How awful!

SMITH: That's okay, Claudia. Last week, this week, what difference does it make? We can celebrate any time. Besides, it's all part of the scheme—-

CLAUDIA: Scheme? Whose scheme? What scheme? I don't like the word.

SMITH: Game, then—

CLAUDIA: What game? Who are the players?

SMITH: You, myself, everybody...

CLAUDIA: Well, in that case (Gets up) Players need energy. So let's have a little food before the boys come back and gobble it all up. (Calls to the kitchen) Roberta!

SMITH: Roberta? Who's that? Another member of the family?

CLAUDIA: Oh no! Just a part-time helper I hired for today. Just for you, Fred.

ROBERTA: Yes, Mrs. Hershey—

CLAUDIA: You can bring in a tray or two of those hot appetizers. We might as well get a head start.

ROBERTA: (From the kitchen) Yes, Mrs. Hershey.

SMITH: (Gets up) No, it cannot be. No, no. Too much of a coincidence. Still, the voice is the same. (Turns and goes toward kitchen door just as Roberta enters with two trays. She wears stylish dress but also kitchen apron and yellow headband) Robbie—I thought I recognized your voice. What on earth are you doing here?

CLAUDIA: (Gets up) What was that? What did I hear? Robbie? So you two know each other. (Display of emotion)

SMITH: Yes, we do, as a matter of fact. Roberta works at the Midtown Plaza.

CLAUDIA: Works? As what? In what capacity?

SMITH: As a maid. What a coincidence to meet her here!
How each day can be full of surprises! (Roberta
says nothing, looks for a minute at Smith and
Claudia. Puts trays on table, returns to kitchen)

CLAUDIA: Full of them. You can say that again! (Walks back
and forth while curtain closes for a brief pause.

❧ ACT III, SCENE 2 ❧

As curtain opens, Sam, Claudia, Smith and Celia are celebrating. Dance music.

CELIA: (Sits on sofa and bangs her cane on the floor in time to music) Nice of you to invite me. I wish I could still dance, the way I used to. (All take turns dancing and changing partners. Celia joins in)

CLAUDIA: Anything else you'd like, Mother?

CELIA: Yes, more food, if you don't mind. (Sits down)

SAM: (To Smith. Effusive) Well, Smith. What do you think? Tell me what you think. (Pause. Smith says nothing) Well, then I tell you want I think. Did you notice what just happened? My mother bangs her cane on the floor and my wife does what she is told. No fuss. No argument.

SMITH: Come now, Sam. Don't tell me you still need a club to show everybody who's the man in the house. By the way, how was your golf game?

SAM: Lousy. High eighties before I stopped counting. But actually I don't really care about scores. Seventies, eighties, nineties. Just figures, not even of money—

SAM: Right. But I have finally persuaded myself not to

consider golf scores as a sign of success, if you know what I mean.

SMITH: In that case you might probably lose your playing partners. People don't normally associate with losers.

SAM: What I really care about now is the time after a game.

SMITH: Après golf—to borrow a phase from winter sports. Common thing now.

SAM: Let's not be devious. I mean the bar. Always open for action, summer or winter. (Confidentially) Some helper Claudia hired for this party. Have you noticed?

SMITH: The maid? Yes, I noticed her. Nice figure.

SAM: Maybe Claudia wants to give me new ideas?

SMITH: You mean fantasies? Don't be silly, Sam. Claudia wouldn't do that sort of thing. She's your wife, the mother of your children. And she loves her family.

SAM: Sure, she does. But love to her means control. Children, husband, kitchen, garden, everything has to be controlled. Everything must be gripped like wood in a vise to be shaped and chiseled.

SMITH: Everything?

SAM: Except Celia, perhaps. She is already too chiseled and shaped by time and experience.

SMITH: The vise grip of experience. That sounds a little grim, especially right now.

SAM: Why? (Kitchen door opens. Enters Claudia and

Roberta with birthday cake. Singing 'Happy
Birthday...' etc.)

SMITH: That's why, I guess. Another year gone by,
another year older.

CLAUDIA: That's right, Fred. Older and wiser (Places cake
on table) Now blow! (Smith blows out most of the
candles, rest are blown out by Roberta. They
exchange looks) Now cut! (Claudia hands Smith
a knife)

SAM: Oh, never mind all this ceremony. Let's have a little
fun first. (Turns up music. Starts dancing
with Roberta)

CELIA: (Bangs cane on floor) Me too! Me too! (Gets up
shakily and tries a few dance steps)

SAM: Permit me, Mrs. Hershey. After all, we've known
each other for some time now. (He takes Celia's
arm and they do a few slow dance steps. Celia
continues to pound floor with her cane. This goes
on for a short time. Enter Brian through
front door)

BRIAN: (Slams book on table) Good afternoon, everybody.
May I join the party? (He turns up stereo, goes to
Claudia, bows formally. They dance also. Lively
dance—improvisations by all)

SMITH: (Guides Celia back to sofa where she collapses.
Goes to stereo which he turns down to a whisper.
Dims lights. Steps up on a chair. Robert exits to
kitchen) Thank you, thank you, everybody. A

wonderful surprise, a fine party. For me, the
mystery uncle, the traveler, the man of means,
supposedly. But no more of that today. (Drinks)
Today I want to be just your friend. But perhaps
that's not so easy, after all. Friendship is a matter
of mutual feelings, isn't it? (Pause) So let's at least
be friendly, let's drink to friendliness. (Somewhat
unsteady on the chair) Goodwill to all—(Jumps
from chair)

CLAUDIA: And to love—

BRIAN: Good heavens! This is sounding more and more
like—a Christmas party. All we need now is a
Santa Claus! (Loud shriek from the kitchen.
Kitchen door is thrown open. Roberta rushes in,
 in panic)

ROBERTA: There's—there's a man—or something—some
body—like a scarecrow—

SAM: Like a scarecrow? Where?

ROBERTA: In there, in the kitchen. Came in through the back
door. Looks like—

SMITH: (Goes over to Roberta, puts his arm around her)
Like what?

ROBERTA: Like what? Like a town drunk. (Acts out) Like
in the movies. That's what he looks like. (More
convulsive acting while Smith tries to restrain her)
And he doesn't say a word. Just comes in through
the back door. Sees the food trays and helps
himself. Starts eating—

SAM: An intruder! I'll go to the bedroom phone and call the police. (Exits quickly. Kitchen door opens slowly. Enter like a guest of the party, the tramp, Richard Brown in disguise)

BROWN: (After a pause) I—apologize for the intrusion. Don't be frightened by my appearance. I'm quite harmless as Mr. Smith will confirm. No gun, no violence, just words.

SMITH: And what brought you here?

BROWN: Hunger, for one thing. It always hits me worst in the afternoon. It's a little better now. I had something in the kitchen just now—

SMITH: So that agreement with yourself—no money collected, no food that day—it's of no value. Just words, right?

BROWN: Sometimes, yes. So, if I could just get the money from you right now, I'll leave as quickly as I came. And no harm done, just another little surprise for this party.

SMITH: Sure! Here's the money. Twenty dollars, right.? Unless all of this is some kind of illusion? A bad dream perhaps? (Takes money from his wallet, hands it to Brown, goes back to Roberta. Sam returns from bedroom)

SAM: Now, will somebody explain to me what this is all about? Who is this—tramp, this—party crasher?

BROWN: The name? You want my name? That's easy. Brown, Richard Brown. And then you want an explanation? Of what? My appearance? Hunger, poverty—they can be explained only through experience. Personal experience. Words mean nothing here. Ask your friend, Mr. Smith. I spoke to him not too long ago. But perhaps he's already forgotten. Perhaps to him I'm just like an actor on a stage, acting out a part before departing. But for myself—this part at least is more like a dream. (Pause, silence)

VOICE: (From outside, very loud) Let me go! Let me go, I said! This is my home!

BROWN: (Quickly) And let _me_ go too. Thanks again for the food. And for the money Mr. Smith. And now good-bye, everybody. Perhaps we'll meet again some day! (Exits smoothly through kitchen door. Commotion at front door. Enter Policeman dragging John Hershey along with him)

POLICEMAN: Caught you, didn't we? Fancy clothes and all. Well, folks, we got here as fast as we could after getting your phone call. Seems we were right on time. Stopped him at the front door, just as he was about to intrude on you!

CLAUDIA: (And Sam) On no! No, no! This is a mistake. This is not an intruder! This is our son John! (General confusion) Oh No-No, my baby! I'm so glad you're back. (Pushes Policeman) Let him go, mister! He lives here!

POLICEMAN: What do you mean? Is this some kind of joke?

SAM: No, of course not. We wouldn't play a joke on our valiant police department. This is John Hershey, our son. He was coming home from our club where they had a special party. Everybody was supposed to dress up as a hobo or tramp. Like Halloween, sort of—

POLICEMAN: So there's no intruder, right? I must write that down in my official report, you know. (Takes out notebook and writes. General confusion continues)

SAM: Right, Officer. There's no intruder. We made a mistake. It was an illusion. We're just not used to seeing one of our family dressed in such clothes.

CLAUDIA: Somehow, this outfit doesn't fit him. Don't you see?

POLICEMAN: No, no. I don't see it! Not really! But if this young person here is your son, if he lives here and belongs here, my work is done. Let me just finish my preliminary report. (Writes. All now step toward backstage in couples: Sam-Claudia, Smith-Roberta, Brian-Celia. Curtain begins to come down, slowly) And you, young tramp, I need a statement from you, too.

JOHN: About our party at the club?

POLICEMAN: About everything.

JOHN: The idea was that all tennis players would dress up like tramps or hobos. Everybody had to wear some old, ragged clothes and long pants.

POLICEMAN: To play tennis?

JOHN: Yes, to play tennis. So everybody would be more like everybody else, and the chances of winning might be more equal.

POLICEMAN: Wouldn't work, young man! The better players would still be better.

JOHN: Of course. But then, another condition of our special game was that no player could use his regular playing arm. Right-handers would be lefties and the other way around.

POLICEMAN: Interesting idea! But did it work?

JOHN: It was fun. Those who usually lose won a little more, and the winners lost. Or at least pretended to. Can't you see the scene? Our club courts all occupied by tramps? The poor playing the game of the affluent? A real spectacle. People stopped and just shook their heads. But it was lots of fun, as I said.

POLICEMAN: And then you came home and got caught!

JOHN: That's right. Variatio delectat, as we learned in Latin class.

POLICEMAN: (Writing again) And how do you spell that?

JOHN: (Takes off his tramp clothes) But now I am myself again! And life can return to normal, I guess. (Curtain had almost gone down to stage floor. Now it goes up again. Cast applauds John. End of play)

✳ The Accounting ✳

Personae:

Mrs. Stone, founder and owner of a specialty store
Bert and Jack Stone, her sons
Bess, Bert's wife
Their two children, ages between eight and twelve
Barbara, clerk in Mrs. Stone's store
Lili and Eric, Barbara's children
Mr. Drossel, an attorney
Two policemen, store customers, undertakers

Acts I and III take place in Stone's General Store which is located in a large cosmopolitan city, Act II in Barbara's apartment.

The action, dominated by Mrs. Stone, develops around her impending death and its effect on her natural and extended family.

The two children have for the most part silent roles. They enter with their parents and immediately use their grandmother's store goods for actions like masquerades or mimicry. They need not be present for the entire play.

❧ THE ACCOUNTING ❧

Cast

I. Major Characters:

BERT STEIN: younger son of Mrs. Stone; a teacher

BESS STEIN: Bert's wife

BARBARA BUTTONTROTTER: clerk in Mrs. Stone's store

MRS. STONE: founder and proprietor of Stone's General Store

ERIC TRABER: part-time employee

JACK STONE (alias St. Pierre): older son of Mrs. Stone

MR. DROSSEL: a lawyer

LILI (LIEBESLEID) TRABER: Eric's half sister

II. Minor Characters:

Act I: Two Policemen

Two men from Dunne's Mortuary

Act III: Customer I (man)

Customer II (woman or man)

Place

A store in a large cosmopolitan city. Shelves and counters, many items of different appeal and value. After the curtain rises there should be a pause for "viewing." Then enter Bert and his wife, Bess, each carrying a suitcase or bag. Newspapers protrude from coat pockets. A doorbell rings as they enter.

BERT: Some trip—quiet and smooth, but—how I hate
night travel, especially on noisy, smoky airplanes.

BESS: Oh, it wasn't so bad. And besides, the plane was
half empty, anyhow.
(She walks to one of the counters)

BERT: That's easy for you to say. You can sleep in any old
place, and even one of the engine pods wouldn't
be too noisy for _you_. Me, I'm bushed, done in,
kaput, and I'm going to sit down
(Falls into a chair)

BESS: Hey—look at this. (She holds up a long, thin item)
Feels like—dried up leather. Wonder what it could
be. Skin of a rattlesnake, maybe?

CLERK: (Rises from behind the counter where she had
been working) Serpens benomenis crotalus—
American rattlesnake, to be precise—And how
may I help you, madam?

BESS: (Drops skin and jumps back) How you startled
me. How—who are you?

CLERK: Barbara Buttontrotter—_Mrs._ Buttontrotter, at
your service. What can I do for you? Did you take
a look around?—Madam?—Sir?

BERT: Yes, _one_ look—it's enough. (He yawns, then

chair trying to sleep)

CLERK: We have—everything, just about—skins and peels, snakes and rats—and our specialty: shells —(She holds up samples of each item, then continues, aggressively) Well, have a look around —or did you already see something, or find something you like?

BESS: (impatient) Yes—No—I mean: see—yes, find— no. You certainly do have a selection of strange things—(She picks up and examines various items)

CLERK: (Who has been following Bess around) How about this lovely shell—Strongylocetrotus drobachiensis —from Tahiti—very beautiful and very cheap—just 15.40—a lovely shell—guaranteed not to explode (She grunts a laugh)—my private little joke, if you pardon me. Well, you like it? Or perhaps some- thing else. What are you looking for, anyhow?

BERT: (Speaking from under his hat, slow but clear and loud) Mother—my mother—

CLERK: Mother? Beg your pardon—did you say 'mother'?

BERT: Yes—I did.

CLERK: Well—we do have many things. But—mother, I'm afraid we do _not_.

BERT: (Pushes his hat back) Yes, you do. This is Stone's General Store, right?

CLERK: Yes, sir.

BERT: Well, what we want is to see—Mrs. Stone, the

proprietor, my mother. Where is she? Has she gone out?

CLERK: Oh—I understand now. You are—Mr. Stone. You are the—

BERT: (Interrupting) Not Stone—Stein—S-t-e-i-n and this is my wife, Bess—

CLERK: Oh, pardon me, Mr. Stone—I mean Mr. Stein—but which Mr. Stein—I mean Stone—which one are you? The -

BERT: (Interrupting again) Bert—the younger of the two. We just flew in, this morning—

CLERK: I see, Mr. Stone—pardon me, Stein—Of course, your mother—I'll go and tell her—

BESS: Didn't she tell you we were coming? Didn't she inform you that—

CLERK: No, madam, not a word. I'm sure she'll be as surprised as I am—you just sit here. I'll go and tell her. (Exits quickly through side door)

BESS: Strange that your mother shouldn't have told her of our coming—her of all people. The way she always wrote to us—this woman, this Mrs. Tutton —whatever, is practically a fixture in this store—

BERT: Yes, strange—but then, my mother always was a strange person. After I was born, she once told me, she took me to the nursery to present me to my other brother Jack who, as she put it, made a terrible face and said: 'Give me this thing.' 'Why?' she asked him. 'So I can throw it out of the window,' he screamed. (Bert pushes his hat back into his face and leans back in chair just as Mother enters wearing a long colorful robe)

MOTHER: Good morning, children—Bess, Bert. I hope you had a pleasant trip? Have you been here long? I came as soon as Barbara told me...

BESS: (Confused) No, we didn't—I mean, yes, we did have a pleasant trip, and we didn't have to wait too long. Your assistant, Mrs. Butter or Button, or whatever—

MOTHER: (Forcefully correct) Buttontrotter—Barbara Buttontrotter ...

BESS: Right—well, she gave us a quick tour of her or rather _your_ store. Interesting place, and some fascinating merchandise—

MOTHER: From all over the world. And I wouldn't be surprised to hear that Barbara also tried to sell you something, right away.

BESS: Yes, she did—this shell (She picks it up) for 15.40—

MOTHER: (With a gesture of delighted approval) Yes, she is a good businesswoman. Always has been, these past twenty years. Barbara started this store with me, you know. (Walks from counter to counter picking up and showing various items) And now that the business is built up, we...

BESS: You get these things from all over the world?

MOTHER: Yes, the world... (Dreamily) My family—is the world. (Sits down) These things—are my children. I wonder...

Bess: (Sits down also) ...about what?

Mother: I wonder if Jack will be coming—I mean, _when_ he
        will be coming...

Bert: (Jerks forward in his chair, drops hat) Oh no—are
        you expecting him, too? You didn't tell us...

Mother: (Softly) I'm always expecting Jack. A mother
        always expects her oldest—so, please, don't get
        excited. You couldn't possibly understand...

Bert: (Agitated) You mean to tell me you sent him the
        same telegram? (Pulls paper from his coat pocket,
        reads) 'Matter of great urgency. Come to see me
        immediately. Mother' (Doorbell rings)

Mother: (Softly, wraps her robe tightly around herself) Of
        course, I did.

Bess: Well, would you mind telling us what the
        'urgency' consists of? Why did you want us to
        come, both of us, right away? It's a long trip,
        you know—(Back door opens, Barbara enters,
        carrying a big box, whistling or humming)

Clerk: Shells, shells, another shipment of shells, more
        than a hundredof them, just delivered to the
        back door...

Mother: (Warily) And did you pay for them? How much
        was it? 20.30 as usual?

Clerk: Yes, it was—and I paid. Cash on delivery.
        (Hums happily)

MOTHER: Well—unpack them right away, as usual. And be careful, will you—

CLERK: All right, I will. (Takes box behind counter. Rustle of paper, song)

MOTHER: And where were we in our discussion? Ah yes, Jack—when he arrives, I'm sure he will know the answer to our problem. He's always been so versatile—and so widely traveled. I bet he could identify the place of origin for each item in this store. Why—the world has practically become his —his garden...

BERT: (From his chair)... and he's the world's worst gardener. Never stops anyplace long enough to plant—or care for things, or watch them grow.

BESS: (Who had started to say something at the same time as Bert, but had checked herself and let him speak) And—what was that problem you just mentioned, Mom? Does it have something to do with our asking us to come here on such short notice? Don't you think you owe us an explanation?

MOTHER: (Turns to face Bert and Bess) Yes, I do, Bess. I must give an explanation to both of you, and I will. But first, I want to reply to what you said, Bert. You were right about your brother Jack. He's no gardener—although he has probably done his man's share of planting—But I didn't like the way you said it, Bert. Your tone of voice. You are always attacking your brother, charging—(Bert

sits up in chair and opens his mouth to speak, but
Mother silences him with an imperious gesture)
Besides—who really needs gardeners in our day
and age? Some city parks, maybe, or some rich
estates. On the whole, gardeners are things of the
past. Man grows steel now, skyscrapers,
rocket launchers—

BERT: (Interrupting) Well—in that case, Jack should have
been in some kind of construction business—a
mechanic perhaps, or an engineer. Too bad, he
could never stay in school long enough, either, to
complete his education—

MOTHER: Oh, he did all right. Probably makes more money
now than all of us combined. And besides we can
not all be—professors, married to schools, as you
are, Bert. (Bert winces and wants to talk, but again
Mother silences him) As for _your_ question, Bess—
why did I send a telegram and ask you two to
come and see me—the answer is simply that—I've
decided to—quit—sell out, retire—perhaps sell the
business to somebody like—Jack, —or to you and
Bert. I don't know yet. That's why I asked you to
come. I want to discuss it with you—with all of
you—(When she said 'quit', Barbara, who had
just unpacked a beautiful shell, stopped humming.
She's held the shell in both hands, and when
Mother is at the end of her speech, she drops it.
Loud crash. Bert jumps up to help Barbara)

CLERK: Oh dear—and such a beautiful specimen. Might have brought in 50—

MOTHER: You could have been more careful, you know.

CLERK: I'm sorry, Mrs. Stone. You know how careful I've always been, all these years. It was just the shock of what you said—about quitting, selling out. Oh dear, what am I going to do?

MOTHER: Oh, stop your lamenting. We're going to discuss everything in detail. That's why I asked my family to come—to discuss things—Right now, however, I must go out and do a little shopping. (Gets up) Want to come along, Bess? You, Bert, can stay and help Buttontrotter clean up. We'll be right back— (She takes a shawl and shopping bag, and makes for the door. Barbara, interrupting her work, steps in her way)

CLERK: And what will Eric say—what will he do?

MOTHER: (Coldly) Eric—Eric?

CLERK: Yes, Eric. You know how attached he is to the store —*you* know...

MOTHER: (Determined) We'll discuss this problem with him too. All problems have solutions, if you just take the time to discuss them—Eric's coming later today, isn't he? Isn't this his day to prepare lunch for us?

CLERK: (Meekly) Yes, it is, Mrs. Stone—But then, there is the mailman, the milkman, the newspaper boy, the garbage man. They all know us. If we leave, oh dear, what will become of them all? And of all of us?

MOTHER: Oh—stop your whining. You make it appear as if the end of the world were coming. There are other businesses all around us, and all of your friends will survive. There'll always be milk. There'll always be garbage—Right now, I must go and do my shopping. Coming, Bess?

BESS: Yes, Mom, I'm coming. (Mother and Bess leave. Bert and Clerk, alone alone, finish cleaning up. Then he sinks back into his chair. Clerk steps up to a mirror, takes off her smock, also her glasses. She arranges her hair, looks 10 years younger, now wearing tight sweater, shiny skirt)

BERT: (Who has been watching her from his chair) Why are you taking off you smock and glasses? You going out too?

CLERK: No, I am not going out. I'm just changing, that's all. I usually do after Mrs. Stone leaves the store. Sometimes, she leaves me in charge for days. For weeks even, when she is traveling—It makes such a difference, being in charge, being independent—Besides, Eric will be coming soon. He's coming every Wednesday, usually, and sometimes Fridays too, to fix lunch for us. He's such a marvelous cook—short order, if you know what I mean.

BERT: (Sleepily from his chair) I don't really care, right now, any food would do—and sleep.

CLERK: Yes—you do look tired after the night on the plane. Here—let me rub your neck—it always helps. (She steps behind Bert's chair, undoes two buttons of her sweater, massages his neck)

BERT: Thank you. This does feel good. It does help— You don't believe in wasting time, Mrs. Buttonroder. Here, we just met this morning, and in this last half hour—You don't even know me—

CLERK: On the contrary, Mr. Stone. I—the name by the way, is Buttontrotter, Barbara for short—On the contrary, I know you quite well, almost like kind of—relative.

BERT: How's that now?

CLERK: From your mother. She talks about you—often.

BERT: Impossible. You must mean my brother, Jack—

CLERK: On no, Mr. Stone. It's Jack she _dreams_ about—but it is _you_ she talks about.

BERT: Not very flattering comments, I suppose.

CLERK: Wrong again, Mr. Stone. Your mother—shall we say, respects you—that is whenever she talks about you and your family. Of course, she is also very fond of your wife and the children.

BERT: (Grunts) Ah—yes, a little more on the right, please. Yes, right there. I must have strained a muscle sitting in the seat on that plane—

CLERK: But on another point you are quite right, Mr. Stone. I don't believe in wasting time. And it seems to me that we won't have much time left to waste around here, in any case—

BERT: What do you mean?

CLERK: Well—if your mother really means to quit—retire
or sell out, I'll have to look out for myself again.
One never knows—

BERT: So, that's want you meant. You are right, of
course, Mrs. Butter—excuse me, but I forget again.

CLERK: Buttontrotter—Barbara, if you please. (She drags
an old footstool over to his chair and places his
feet on it) It's not my real name (Confidentially) In
fact, your mother made it up, sort of. She—
translated it.

CLERK: (Has taken off one of Bert's shoes and begins to
massage his foot) My name? It is—I mean it was—
Swain, Barbara Swain, until I took the name of
my—husband. He was an immigrant, worked in
a restaurant, loved to eat—what a man he was, oh,
what a man—Hans Knopftraber was his name—

BERT: (Repeats, clearly) Knopftraber.

CLERK: Well—after—I mean, after a while, I began to
think I should find out what it would be like to be
called Mrs. Knopftraber—but when I told Mother
—excuse me, _your_ mother what my new name
would be, she said this would be impossible. It
was a German name, and _such_ a German name,
and she herself had changed hers right after the
war. I can still see her, Mr. Stone. She was standing
right by that mirror. She shook her head and said:

'Knopftraber—this will never do! We'll have to anglicize it.' And right then and there she translated the name into Buttontrotter—and that's what I have been since. Often I felt like shortening the name to either Button or Trotter—but I couldn't decide which one of the two was better. Anyway—everybody calls me just Barbara—(She undoes another button and goes to work on Bert's other foot)

BERT: And Hans, your husband, what became of him?

CLERK: He didn't like the name Buttontrotter—not at all. So—after it happened, he left me. And here I am, have been for twenty years or so—Are you feeling better now? You look better—don't we women have our ways?

BERT: After _what_ happened?

CLERK: After Eric was born.

BERT: (Grunts) I see—Yes, and I do feel better, thank you. Now if we could only have a little food—(He takes his shoes over to a sofa, sits down, puts shoes back on) By the way, where did you learn this—massaging people?

CLERK: I used to be a nurse, and as a specialty, part-time, I took up this massage work, the feet primarily—

BERT: Some kind of job you picked there.

CLERK: Oh—you get used to it. (Sits down beside Bert) As you get used to everything, after a while. Besides the work has an interesting sideline—

BERT: So? What kind?

CLERK: (Seriously) From the shape of people's feet a skilled masseuse can tell what kind of people they are and what ails them—

BERT: A kind of amateur diagnosis? You don't mean it!

CLERK: But I do. In fact, I used to be so good in diagnosing illnesses that more and more customers came back to me just for that reason— until the doctors in town became jealous and made me quit...

BERT: I suppose now you could say something about my feet too, right?

CLERK: Not too much right now, I'm afraid. I didn't really have enough time. But, if you want me to try again... (She moves closer to him)

BERT: No, thank you—not right now...

CLERK: You seem healthy to me, healthy enough, but lonely.

BERT: You think so?

CLERK: I do. Must be lonely, sort of—I mean—to be married to the same person, all the time—

BERT: (Shifting to corner of sofa) Lonely? You're wrong there. Married to Bess—with our children? Lonely? No, definitely not.

CLERK: (Shifting also) Monotonous, then—

BERT: What are you driving at?

CLERK: (With forced laugh) Driving—me? I never learned to drive. I like to leave that to the man—

—Would you?

BERT: What?

CLERK: Drive—ride—with me—

BERT: (Puts his arm around her, protectively) You are a good woman, Barbara. But, as you just said—leave the driving to the man—

CLERK: (Leaning her head back against sofa) Ah—that's what I like. Nothing like getting paid promptly—(At this moment, guitar strums are heard from outside. Voice of a man singing) Eric—good heavens—he, already?

BERT: Well—you _were_ expecting him, right?

CLERK: Yes, but not quite so soon. Not right now! (Eric enters. About 17, long hair but clean, dressed exotically. Sings and strums as he enters)

Eric (Briefly surveys the scene, then stops playing and singing) Good day everybody. I didn't disturb you, did I? Or perhaps I should play and sing a little more? (He strums again, picks up interrupted song)

CLERK: No, you didn't disturb us. Come right in. I was expecting you, anyhow.

BERT: You make nice music. Perhaps we can hear a little more? Later?

ERIC: No. Right now. Why not? (Sits down and plays a piece, flamenco, classical or improvisation. Bert and Clerk lean back and listen)

BERT: (After Eric finishes) Bravo—and thank you, young man. Where did you learn to play so well? And

your instrument—such a full sound! Oh—by the
way, I'm Bert—Bert Stein, Mrs. Stone's son. She
and my wife have gone out to do some shopping.
We just arrived here, a little while ago—

ERIC: Please to meet you, sir. (He plays a little more)
Where I learned to play? Mostly, I taught myself.
Music has been—my home, in a way, for as long as
I can remember. That is the home of my soul, my
better self. Recently, I've also begun to
give lessons.

CLERK: (Who has meanwhile put her smock back on) Yes
—but right now, you may get to work on the lunch,
as always. Mrs. Stone will be back shortly, and
she'll bring the food. (Eric shrugs his shoulders,
puts his guitar and begins to set a pot and frying
pan on a small electric stove. Soon, doorbell rings
and Mother and Bess return. Both carry bags of
groceries. Animated talk)

BESS: (Setting her bag on counter) What a day it is outside, what a beautiful day for shopping. (To Bert)
Oh, Bert, I'm so glad now we came. I really like
this town—and this store. (Looking around, she
sees Eric) And this must be Eric—So nice of you
to come today—and already busy working for us.
Good boy!

MOTHER: We bought all the food we need. Here's the
bacon, Eric. And some fish—fresh flounder,
very good!

BERT: And—did you get some beer?

BESS: (Chattering gaily while unpacking) I wanted to
          buy some. I told Mom You always liked a bottle,
          especially with fish. Your father usually had some
          beer with his lunch, you said...

BERT: So—did you get some?

BESS: No.

BERT: Why not?

BESS: Mother said not to.

MOTHER: Alcohol and business don't mix! I won't have
          drinking in this store. We bought Coke instead,
          plenty of it, for everybody. (She sees clerk
          standing beside mirror) Good heavens, Barbara,
          what did you do with your glasses?

CLERK: I—took them off. I'm wearing my contacts.

MOTHER: I see—Expecting one of your favorite customers,
          perhaps? Or were you trying to sell something
          else to Bert while we were out? (Turns to Bert) She
          did—didn't she? (Clerk steps in front of the
          mirror, begins to remove contacts)

BERT: Oh, for heaven's sake, Mother. Be sensible. You
          were only gone for a short time. Mrs. Buttontrotter
          was—very nice. —And Eric, too. He sang and
          played for us. Beautiful.

CLERK: Yes, he did. The boy has talent. And he always
          says that his guitar is his best possession.

BERT: But—I still don't see why we couldn't have a little
          beer—

MOTHER: Because—

BERT: Because my father always had some with his lunch. Isn't that right?

MOTHER: (Angry) Your father has nothing to do with it. You will leave him out of this, you hear—and out of this store. And you should know better than trying to bait me—(Clerk screams)

CLERK: Help me, somebody. I lost one of my lenses. Help me. (Eric rushes in Clerk's direction, but Bess waves him back)

BESS: Stay in your places, everybody. Don't move. You might step on the lens. Don't move. (She gets down on hands and knees, crawls over to Clerk)

BERT: For heaven's sake, Bess. Not on your hands and knees. You are going to ruin your stockings. Don't do it, Bess!

MOTHER: Let her search, Bert, and leave her alone, she's just trying to help.

BESS: Here it is! Found it! Here's you lens, Barbara.

CLERK: Ah, thank you, thank you!

MOTHER: (To Bert) See—I told you to leave her alone.
(To Bess) Bess, you're wonderful!
(To Eric) Go on with your cooking, Eric—
(To Bert) Well—we've got all the food we need, even if your brother should come in right now.

BERT: In that case, you should have brought food for two more people, at least—

MOTHER: What do you mean?

BERT: Well—Jack is always a few steps ahead of the police, isn't he? And one of these times he's going to come—with the police right behind him— (Sarcastic) and they'll probably be very hungry after the chase—

CLERK: (Has put her glasses back on, and is now helping Eric) Right you are, Mr. Stone. That is exactly what is going to happen one day. Last time Mr. Jack came, he took one of our best alligator skins—took it from right over there He never paid for it, and never sent it back—

MOTHER:(Annoyed) Oh—stop it, Barbara. I gave him that skin—and anyhow we'll take this hurdle when we get to it—

BERT: If—

MOTHER: How's the food coming, Eric?

ERIC: Just a little while longer. I am doing the fish now. Just a few more minutes. (He puts fish into the pan, then takes his guitar and plays or sings a little while curtain falls.)

❧ ACT I, SCENE 2 ❧

Same scene, about 10 minutes later. As curtain rises, Bert, Bess, Mother and Clerk are sitting around small table. Eric is serving the food.

MOTHER: As I explained to Bess while we were out shopping, the store is in good shape. We have a central location and steady clientele. The season from October to January has been especially properous these last few years.

BESS: Yes—I think it would be fascinating to have—I mean, to run a store offering so many different goods and services to so many people. Wouldn't it, Bert? Why—it would almost be like—teaching school, with all these customers coming in, and you—I mean, we—all of us, explaining different items, prices, quality—

BERT: (Pulling a bone from his plate and holding it up for examination) You make it sound very attractive, except I have not seen any people, any customers.

CLERK: Wednesday is usually a slow day. Besides, Mrs. Stone told me to keep the front door locked and put up a sign: closed for the day. Only for today, of course, while we have visitors—My—this fish is good. Is there a little more, Eric?

ERIC: Coming up. (He brings a serving dish to the table and goes first to Mother) Would you like a little more, Mrs. Stone?

MOTHER: No, thank you. I've had enough. (Eric takes dish to Clerk who helps herself, solidly)

BESS: (Speaking to Mother) You've hardly touched your food, Mom. You should eat a little more. Barbara is right. This food is good—(Turns and speaks to Bert) And the children, Bert. I was thinking—they could learn a lot in this store—and help us when they get a little older Don't you think so, Bert?

BERT: They would have this place taken apart in a day, wild as they are. I wonder how they are doing at home—hope the sitter is still alive.

CLERK: Oh, they can't be as bad as all that. With parents like you...

BESS: Bert exaggerates. Besides, educating young people is his profession, and professionals tend to be biased.

BERT: I'm just tired, that's all.

CLERK: Do you have a picture of your children?

BESS: I do. Right here, in my wallet. There—
(She hands photo to Clerk)

CLERK: Charming. Perfect angels.

BERT: In pictures they usually are—like some actors on the screen—

CLERK: (To Mother) Have you seen the picture?

Mother: (Wearily) Yes, I've seen it—you can give it back
    to Bess.

Clerk: (Finishing her plate) This was good food. Could I
    have another bottle of Coke, please?

Bert: (Yawning) Still don't see why I couldn't have a
    little beer—

Bess: Oh, stop being so persistent, Bert. It's almost
    childish of you—

Bert: Childish? And don't I have the right to be childish
    in my mother's presence, practically in her home?
    All children have that right—

Bess: Except that you aren't exactly a child anymore,
    are you?

Mother: He's tired—and perhaps angry with me. We
    should have bought him his beer, after all—
    (speaking to Bert with sudden emphasis) Yes—
    your father used have beer at lunch, and then his
    liquor at night, and then—he went out chasing
    after the girls. Often, I didn't see him for nights in
    a row—

Bert: Yes, I know—you've told me, many times. But I
    still don't see what this has to do with my having
    a little beer, right now, today. (Clerk and Bess
    increasing restless in their chairs)

Mother: With beer—very little, but with your attitude
    quite a bit—(Bert pulls pipe from his pocket stuffs
    it with tobacco from a pouch)

Bess: (To Clerk) Perhaps we should clear the table now.

And then we can have the special dessert (The two
women get up and remove the plates)

BERT: (Lighting the pipe) Attitude? What do you mean?

MOTHER: I mean the same as before. I don't think you
          should bait me with with your father. You know
          very well how I feel. (Turns back to him)

BERT: I'm sorry. I don't mean to bait you—not at all. It's
          just that I've never been able to stand the thought
          of your being all alone—

MOTHER: (Turning to face Bert) I'm not alone. I have my
          store, my work, my travels—

BERT: Yes, you have all that. But for how much longer?
          Besides—that's not really my point.

MOTHER: I don't understand—

BERT: Then I'll try to say it again—in a different way.
          (Heavy puffs) This might strike you as a strange
          thought, but ever since I was a child, I've always
          wanted to see you and my father together,
          just once—

MOTHER: (Coldly) Together? How? Where? Doing what?

BERT: Oh—I don't know—in a house, in a room, in bed
          —at a table, together—

MOTHER: (Sarcastic) Eating together—drinking—
          Beer, perhaps?

BERT: Yes, perhaps. But most of all: living together.
          That's what I mean.

MOTHER: You are dreaming, and you don't know what you
          are saying, Bert. Your father—and God knows I

loved him with all my heart—was mean to me, and cruel—leaving me alone so often, especially after you boys were born.

BERT: Yes, I know. You've told me—

MOTHER: It broke my heart. In more ways than one, it broke my heart—

BERT: Yes—

MOTHER: In more ways than you could ever know. (Silence. Bess and Clerk are are coming back carrying a big cake. They set new plates on table and set the cake in the middle)

CLERK: Here we are. A beauty, right? Let's cut it. Eric, come and join us for a little celebration.

ERIC: Okay, okay, but what are we celebrating? Anybody have a birthday, or something?

BESS: Mine is closest—just three weeks ago, yesterday. (Cuts slices vigorously and puts them on plates)

BERT: Yes, and Margaret's, our little girl's is in less than a month—

CLERK: So—let's start the celebration. What are we waiting for? (She takes smock off, lets hair down)

MOTHER: All right then, let's start. Jack will have his piece when he arrives. Go ahead, everybody, and eat. I've had enough—

CLERK: Enough. Lately, you have been nibbling like a mouse—and by the way, Mrs. Stone, you said you would tell us, one day soon, why you have decided to quit working. Why? So suddenly?

MOTHER: I did promise to tell you—and I really wanted to wait until we are all together. However—you might as well know now, and perhaps tell Jack later, when he comes. —I went to see my doctor a few weeks ago, he told me I may have little time left to live—

BESS: He said _that_? How could he? (Absolute silence)

MOTHER: I asked him to be absolutely truthful with me.

BERT: But—you never told _us_.

MOTHER: I'm telling you _now_.

CLERK: (Gets up, goes to Mother and puts her arms around her, protectively) Mrs. Stone, oh—Mrs. Stone. I had no idea. Can I help you in any way? I used to be a nurse, you know. I was good at diagnosing, too. What did your doctor say? Cancer? Something else?

MOTHER: No, a heart condition. It goes back to my youth when I had rheumatic fever. It was aggravated when the children were born. And just a few months ago, you remember, I fell off a chair, right here in the store. I blacked out, sort of—collapsed. That's when I made the appointment with the doctor. Have had these chest pains and constrictions ever since—

CLERK (Solicitous) And the doctor probably told you to take it easy—rest, and do just a little work, right?

MOTHER: Exactly. But—how can one run a business without work? And—'no excitement,' he said. But what is life without excitement? Why—this has been our whole life here, all these years: work and excitement—right?

CLERK: Right. But now you must change, Mrs. Stone. And don't worry about anything. We'll help you. We'll take care of you. (Eric gets up, takes his guitar, goes to back of store and sings softly)

BERT: (Gets up, too) You should have told us before, Mother. All this is so—unexpected, so sudden—

MOTHER: Unexpected? Sudden? You are right. But then— death often is—

BESS: (Who has followed Bert) Don't worry, Bert. We'll talk everything over, later on. Things will be all right, you'll see. Later, later—(Silence, then a sudden pounding on front door. Eric opens it. Enter Jack Stone: stylish but careless dress. Swarthy attempts at elegance. After Eric has locked front door, Jack circles table while everybody gets back into chairs. All look at Jack with kind of awe)

MOTHER: (First to speak, clutching her chest) Jack, oh, Jack, it's you. I knew you would come, I knew it all along—didn't I say so, everybody?

JACK: Yes, Mommy (Kisses her tenderly) You rang for me, and here I am. And—what have we here? A little family party? Why—even our learned professor has climbed down from his ivory tower. Why—this must be a special event. Good after—

noon, everybody—Bess (Kisses her hand) Eric, and
Barbara, dear. (Kisses her suggestively. She pulls
back a little but does not exactly resist) And what
do I smell? Fish? Fried Fish?

ERIC: Yes, Mr. Jack—fried fish.

JACK: Excellent, excellent—some of your wonderful
cooking, Eric. (Looks around) And cake—just
sliced—are we celebrating? A wedding? A birthday? Yours, Barbara, my dear? Well—whatever—
at least I got here in time for dessert—But, hold it!
Why no drinks? Nothing except these few bottles
of Coke? Half filled yet. We'll have to change that,
right away. (Mother and Bess raise their hands in
silent protest, but Jack disregards them) Eric, go to
the liquor store at the corner. Here (Writes on
two Gordon's, two Canadian Club—some soda
water—this will do for now. Have them charge it
to the store—(Eric takes paper and leaves by side
door) I have come, Mommy, as you asked. And
later on, we'll all have a talk. But first, let's finish
this party in style. (He takes Eric's guitar and
strums a few chords while curtain falls)

❧ ACT I, SCENE 3 ❧

As curtain rises, Jack is sitting on the counter, playing guitar and singing. Others sit around table. Clinking of glasses.

BERT: (To Mother) You shouldn't have let him order all this liquor. You should have stopped him.

MOTHER: (Raising her glass) Oh—let him have it his way. He's such good company. I am sure he will pay for what he ordered—eventually. He will also help us with our problem, simply through the magic of his presence—And how much he resembles his father when he sings and plays. How much he acts like him—

BERT: But—I thought you wanted to forget—or at least not be reminded—

MOTHER: Yes, forget—but not right now, please not right now. Let's have a little more to drink, first—Here, everybody, drink up. (More drinks are poured)

BERT: Still, I don't like the expense—and in the middle of the day, too. Besides, you should take it easy, Mother. You just told us—(He gets up and goes to where Jack is sitting) I'm glad you came, Jack. For Mother's sake, I'm glad. But—just take it easy —okay? Mother is not feeling too well today. She has been to the doctor. She told us a little while ago, just before you came in. In fact, she said—

JACK: (Interrupts, jumps off counter, circles table again, then shouts at Bert across the table) I thought you had quit school for just one day—Or can you never stop nagging—nagging and finding fault. Will you not stop it, not even once in your life, your eternal schoolmastering? In any case stop telling _me_ what to do, you hear?

BERT: (Conciliatory, but determined) I wasn't trying to tell you anything. I was just asking a simple favor of you, that's all. (Bess gets up and stands next to Bert) Stop being the actor, Jack. You are not on stage, right now—

JACK: (Surprised) On stage? Who—I? I wish I were. But —here? Or where else? Caracas? Mexico City? Paris? (Recites grandly) 'All the world's a stage...' as somebody said. Okay, I'll accept that, Mr. Somebody, and this world is my stage, right now—(Everybody has become silent as they watch the two brothers, especially Jack)

BERT: It isn't just Mr. Somebody, Jack—

JACK: So, there you go again—correcting, nagging, lecturing—go and correct your damn papers, will you—and leave me _alone_—

BERT: Oh, knock it off, will you? I was just trying to set things straight. No nagging was intended. (Jack goes to another counter, opens a drawer, takes out a heavy bullwhip of western American origin)

JACK: But—you've always done it, you've always nagged me—and you, you were the one who did things right, especially in school—the typical do-it-right Mr. Knowall, you were. (Beats the counter with whip) But now, look at you—what has become of you? A schoolmaster—a nagging pedant—that's what you _are_ (Points whip at Bert)

MOTHER: (Tries to get up but is held back in chair by Clerk) Oh, stop it, the two of you. Not that again, not right now—please (All are silent for a second)

BERT: Schoolmaster—okay, have it that way. And I am proud of it. It's vocation, my life. Just as _your_ life, Mother, is this store—and your life, Jack—well? What _is_ your life? The stage? The world? The whip? (Takes a few steps towards Jack, but Bess restrains him) Let me just tell you a little more, just a little—A schoolteacher of today is quite different from what he used to be—the kind you had so much trouble with. Many people still think that all a teacher has to do is know his lessons and keep order. Well—far from it. Today's youth is different, today's schools are different. Today's youngsters are troubled by much more than lack of knowledge and fear of examinations. Our age is —shaky, and so are all of us living in this age. Most of us older people have learned to hide their fears, or compensate for them—but the youth—they express their feelings openly. They make no pretenses—(Jack has gone back to counter. He puts down the whip, picks up guitar, starts playing and singing, quietly) We of the older generation —we live in fear, mostly fear of change— but the younger people live in fear of fear itself. And that is a real death spiral—And the teacher? Where does _he_ stand? Right in the middle—right in the current of time. He is like a stepping-stone between the generations. He is like—a man running a ferry from shore to shore—from past to present, from present to future, from child to parent—always steering across rapids and deep currents, always expected to be steady, undeterred—and always in the same boat with his young passengers, his charges—that's what today's schoolmaster is like—he is like a ferryman —a ferryman—

JACK: (Strums loud, beats heels against counter) Ha-ha— did you hear that, all of you—a ferryman. Brother Bert has become a ferryman. We must sing to that— your long list of achievements—Come on now, all together—(Signs with exaggerated accent) Ist das nicht ein ferryman? Ja, das ist ein ferryman. (Jack jumps off counter, begins to dance, but suddenly there is a strong knock on front door. Eric gets up, opens door, sudden silence, except for voices at door. Eric locks door, returns)

ERIC: Two men are outside. They want to speak with the

proprietor of the store.

MOTHER: (Gets up slowly) All right. Who are they? Police?

(Jack jumps off counter and disappears behind it)

MOTHER: (Unlocks front door) Yes—what can I do for you, gentlemen? We are not open for business today— you see the sign—(Two men enter)

FIRST MAN: Sorry to trouble you, ma'am. Is this the General Store, 16 Manet Street?

MOTHER: Yes, it is—sorry, we are in such confusion. A little family party—My son Bert, his wife Bess, Eric Traber and Mrs. Buttontrotter, my assistants. I am the proprietor—

SECOND MAN: (Looking around the store, consulting a small address book) This must be the wrong address. We are looking for a music store.

FIRST MAN: I see many different things here, but no music, no instruments.

CLERK: None, but Eric's guitar. Where is it, anyhow? Oh, there, on the counter. But—

MOTHER: But—it's isn't for sale—

FIRST MAN: I am sorry we have troubled you, ma'am. Pardon our intrusion—and good afternoon to all of you. (They leave)

BESS: I wonder who they were, and what they were really looking for—

MOTHER: Oh—we get all kinds of surprise customers. You never can tell. (All sit down)

CLERK: The other day, somebody came in looking for an

army outfit—General Store, you know—
(nervous laughter)

BERT: By the way, where is Jack? Did he bring any
luggage? We ought to—

JACK: (Appearing from behind the counter) At the
airport. I left it there so I could get here as soon
as possible—

BERT: I see. We must not forget to pick it up later on—

MOTHER: (Happily) Yes, we must. But right now—let's
finish the champagne. Let's drink up, everybody.
I'm so glad you came, Jack. It was gloomy here
before you arrived. There was no joy—the place
was as morose as an empty funeral parlor—

CLERK: (Pouring more drinks) Of all the beautiful items
we have bought and sold, I think our semi-
precious stones were the most successful. (Goes to
a counter, opens a drawer, takes out a box) People
are just crazy about them. They think they are the
real thing, and they are willing to pay the price.
Imagination, dreams—that's what life is all
about, even in business. And so, the stones never
fail to look attractive to me, too. I have gotten into
the habit of looking at them at least once a day—
more often of course when I show them to
customers. Somehow, these mineral things—
they remind me of—people. And they give me
confidence, they cheer me up. (She has opened the
box and places stones on counter, one by one)

JACK: What cheers you more—stones or customers?

CLERK: Oh, Mr. Jack—the customers, of course, especially when they pay well—(Nervous laughter). Here, now it is done, my own Stonehenge—Want to have your fortune told, Mr. Jack?

MOTHER: Enough of all that. Let's get back to business. Sit down, everybody. Barbara, Eric, you too. (Clerk puts stones back into box, box back into drawer. All sit down) As I explained before you came, Jack, I am going to—retire. I want to take it easy for a while. Somebody else will take over the store—one of you.

JACK: (Excited) This _is_ a surprise. Why the sudden decision?

BERT: Mother is not well, that's why. I tried to explain it to you before. In fact, she must not work at all any longer—just rest, take it easy and—live.

MOTHER: Oh, you make it sound so serious, Bert. I'll last a little longer yet. (To Jack) Jack, you are my oldest son—do you think you could—shrink your wide world a little—into this compact world of four walls? I did myself, long ago. Do you think you could—manage to narrow your—stage a little?

JACK: Me? You mean I should—run this place, this museum? Why—I 'd rather—
          (Gets up and paces floor)

MOTHER: Yes, run it. Own it. You think you can? (There is general commotion. All get up, all except Mother.

BERT: | Eric gets busy with the dishes. Clerk puts her smock back on. Bert and Bess walk into corner)
BERT: She can't be serious. She knows so well that the small world of ordinary things will never hold her Jack. He is convinced he is made for the big world —for all of it.

BESS: I can't understand it either. And after your mother was so nice to me when we went shopping together. Why, she almost offered the place to me —to you and me, that is. She practically begged me to accept it. We even dropped in at her lawyer's office—(Jack has again gone behind counter. He takes whip out of drawer, puts it on counter, then is busy for a while opening other drawers)

MOTHER: Relax, relax, everybody. Why, you are scattering as if a bombshell had exploded right here on the table. Come back everybody, Let's sit down, reason, discuss. (Everybody obeys and sits down) Well, Jack what do you say?

JACK: (Beating palm of his hand with the whip) Sure— I'd take it over. Of course, there will be a lot of changes—papers to sign, authorities are always so fussy—

MOTHER: (Disregards his last remark) And what would you do first, Jack, if you owned the store?

JACK: (Gets up and paces floor again) First? I don't really know. It's all so sudden, I don't know—sell, I guess, sell and buy—buy and sell, just as you have been doing for all these years—But—why do you say 'if you owned the store'? I had the impression that it was all settled. If your health demands it, we should settle the matter right away. I didn't come all this distance to—play the game of 'if', like we used to say as children: if your great-grandmother had four wheels, she'd be a bus... (Nervous laughter from all)

MOTHER: Very well. My lawyer has all the papers. You know where his office is—right down the street, at the next corner. All you have to do, Jack, is go and get them. Of course, there'll be some papers for you to sign, too.

JACK: (Eagerly) Okay—I know where his office is. I'll go and be right back—(He goes to front door, stops there, turns and leaves by back door. All talk at once now)

BESS: How could you do it, Mom? He'll never settle down, and you know it—

BERT: And we didn't really have to come all the way. It had all been settled ahead of time—

ERIC: Coffee anybody? (Moves around) Ah—it's always good to be able to cook up more than just one dish. Variety—that's the secret. (Takes coffeepot and begins to dance around store) Hats (Puts one on) and coats (Picks old long leather coat from rack and puts it on) and now—a sword or dagger (Finds item) and who am I now? Eric the cook?

Eric the part-time assistant? Eric the adventurer—
(Does some shadow fencing) Ah—it's the clothes
that make the difference, even for me—
especially for me—

CLERK: (Shrieks from behind counter) Help, help they are
gone—gone—

BERT AND BESS: (jumping up) Who—what is gone?

CLERK: The stones—from the box. My stones from my box.
Mr. Jack must have taken them, I swear it—

BERT: Wouldn't surprise me—taken them and run.

MOTHER: (Remains in chair) Yes. He probably did. He's
always taken things. Oh well—

BERT: But what are we going to do? Just sit around? I
think we should call the authorities
(Goes to telephone)

MOTHER: No, Bert, no. Don't call, please. Jack will be back.
I _know_ he will be back. (All make various gestures
of disbelief, disgust, despair as curtain falls)

⚜ ACT I, SCENE 4 ⚜

As curtain opens, all characters of the previous scene are sitting around the table. Depressed mood.

BERT: (Gets up and begins to pace floor) He'll never
           come back. First, he didn't bring his luggage from
           the airport. (General nodding of consent, all
           around. Suddenly, back door opens cautiously
           and Jack enters, followed by Lawyer, carrying
           briefcase)
JACK: (Angry but trying to be nonchalant) He wouldn't
           let me sign the papers in his office. He said, the
           signing would have to be done right here—
Lawyer ...in the presence of all the persons concerned.
           Witnesses will be needed too—Good afternoon,
           everybody. I believe, I know everybody except
           (Points) you, sir. (Steps to Bert)
MOTHER: Oh, Mr. Drossel—thank you so much for coming
           along with Jack. I am sorry, you've never met Bert,
           my younger son—I introduced you to Bess, his
           wife, earlier today. Both have come today, as I
           have asked them—
LAWYER: Pleased to meet you, Mr. Stone.
BERT: Stein—Bert Stein.

LAWYER: Stein, excuse me, Mr. Stein—and Mrs. Stein—

MOTHER: Bert never changed his father's name. I did of course, and so did Jack. We anglicized it. Found it ever so much more convenient all around, in business, family—

JACK: We did, didn't we, Mom, you and I. Bert, of course, he wouldn't understand. He never has to adjust to the real world. And why should he? In his school, in his class—well, that's his business, not ours—

LAWYER: (Still looking around the room) And the young gentlemen in the back—I don't recall having had the pleasure of meeting him, either—

MOTHER: Probably not. He does not work full-time. He only comes on occasion to help out and cook for us—

ERIC: (Steps forward) Eric is the name, Eric Traber. Part-time work is my specialty. Cooking, cleaning, love —part-time. I find the variety especially exciting. A new challenge every day, every hour. Survival— it's survival that is reality to me, not philosophy. When I'm done with one chore, I immediately feel that there is something else left to do. No rut for me, no routine. Leave the ruts to the rats; for me, the great challenge is part-time specialization.

LAWYER: An interesting theory, young man. I must remember it—for my—retirement. What did you say your name was?

ERIC: Traber, sir. Eric Traber—and then, there is a

dream that goes with my life—that some day I'll be
able to put all the parts of my work together and
make one whole out of them, and perhaps I'll be
fulfilled, you might say—The Traber, by the way,
is shortened. My birth certificate says Knopftraber
—which I've always found too long, too
complicated, especially for my kind of life. So—I
shortened it, and now my name is sort of part-
time, too. (Nervous laughter)

LAWYER: (Unruffled) Traber—well, I'll try to remember that,
too. Summer will soon be around and we'll have
that avalanche of nonsupport cases. Might need
somebody to do a little—investigating for me,
part-time?

BERT: (Curtly) We didn't really come all the way to
Mother's store to discuss—part-time work, did
we? (During Lawyer's talk with Eric, Clerk had
gradually moved closer to Bert, then had gone
back to her original place)

CLERK: (Meekly) No, we didn't.

JACK: Certainly not.

LAWYER: Right. I agree. (Opens briefcase) Here are the
papers you asked me to draw up, Mrs. Stone. All
ready for you to sign—

JACK: In that case, I don't know why I had to come to
your office at all—

MOTHER: (Quietly) To fetch him, bring him here. We never
knew exactly when you would be coming, Jack—

BESS: (Gets up and makes several steps, in no particular direction. Tries to decide—)

BERT: (Solicitously) Sit down, Bess, please sit down—

BESS: (With sudden resolution, stepping up to Jack) Before we do anything else, Jack—hand over those stones.

JACK: (In false surprise) Stones? What stones?

BESS: The stones you took from the drawer. The stones Barbara had just shown us, a little while before you left. You know exactly what stones—

JACK: (Coldly) If you think I have them, come and search me if you dare. (Bert gets up nervously while Jack slowly retreats to corner of store)

BESS: (Following Jack) These stones belong to—the store. Hand them over them over! Now!

JACK: (Turns to wall and takes an old dagger from a hook, unsheathes it) You'll have to come and get them, first—

BESS: If you think I am afraid of you—I'm not (Advances toward him, some fast pushing action from both, but Jack keeps dagger down)

JACK: (Lunges forward as if to charge at Bess, but he is stopped by Mother who gets up and with quick hand gesture waves Jack back into his corner) We'll see—we'll see.

MOTHER: Stop playing around now, Jack, and let's get to work on these papers.

BESS: (Defiant) I still think he should hand over the

stones, first—

BERT: (Going to her) Not now, Bess, not now—Let's do these papers first, as Mother says. Come now and sit down. (All sit around table)

LAWYER: These are the papers, Mrs. Stone. We can read them together, then sign them, with some of the people present serving as witnesses. (He gives papers to Mother, copies in folders to Jack, Bert, Bess)

JACK: (Reads quickly, aloud)... that said store known as the General Store become the property of the undersigned provided that, and as long as, the undersigned stay in residence in this city and personally manage the store and—(Bert and Bess gasp, Clerk and Eric shift uneasily) the present employees of said store retain their positions unchanged until they desire to leave employment in said store, or die—

(Jack gets up, paces) This sounds like a—bind to me, almost like some kind of contract, between one man and one hundred thousand—things, dead things—a marriage even between myself and these people—in a way (Laughs) like crawling into a shell, with myself as the—snail—

(Sudden decision) okay—I'll sign. I'll sign in a little while, an hour or so, as soon as I get my luggage at the airport. Will that be okay—Mother? Everybody? (He moves toward rear door. Bess jumps up and blocks his way. Shoving by both)

BESS: First, hand over those stones—

JACK: Oh, for crying out—I'll be back, right away. So, get out of my way, will you? (He pushes Bess. She screams. Confusion. Eric advances toward Jack, guitar in hand. Just then, there is a loud rap at front door)

VOICES: Open up, please. This is the police. We have a warrant to search these premises. Open up. (Jack grabs Bess, pulls her with him behind counter, takes dagger from sheath. Bert, Mother, Eric, Clerk all approach the two, but without real determination. Lawyer gathers papers into brief case and goes to front door)

JACK: Okay—stop it, everybody. Stay where you are. This seems to be my day for surprises. Mother—if you don't want this knife in the back of this woman, go to the front door and tell the police that I'm not here. And get rid of them, Mr. Drossel —one more step, and—

MOTHER: So, they're after you, Jack? Are they?

JACK: I suppose so. I eluded their trap at the airport. They were waiting to arrest me after I arrived, but —I shot one of them. Now, they've caught up with me—(Bert advances toward Jack) No, Bert— everybody else, stay where you are. Beside the dagger, I still have my gun—so get back to your seats. And Mother, please—(Again, loud knocks

at front door. Mother walks slowly to front door,
opens it. Two men look through
half-opened door)

FIRST MAN: Excuse me, madam. We believe that a certain
Jack Stone is in this store. We have a warrant for
his arrest. Please step aside...

MOTHER: Stone? Jack Stone? No. You must be mistaken.
Stein—Bert Stein, he is here—my son, in that chair

SECOND MAN: We found Jack Stone's luggage at the
airport, and in it a notebook with this address.
Are you sure he is not here? Sure?

MOTHER: Yes, I'm sure—now, if you don't mind. We are
very busy right now—(She closes front door,
everybody freezes in stunned silence. Suddenly,
both Bert and Eric jump toward Jack. Scuffle, Jack
fends off Bert with dagger. Mother intervenes,
stops Eric from hitting Jack) No, Eric, no. And Jack
—what have you done? There's blood all over your
arm, Bert—(Sudden crash as front door is broken
down. Two men rush in, Jack dives out of back
door. Mother blocks two men, arms outstretched)
Gentlemen—wait, what are you doing? I told you,
he is not here—he is—oh, how it hurts. (Clutches
somebody, please help me. My pills, my drops—
quick, somebody—

FIRST MAN: (Bending over her) Sorry, ma'am, very sorry.
Somebody had better call an ambulance, this
looks bad. Get a doctor, right away. (All crowd

around mother, lift her up and carry her to sofa)

SECOND MAN: And I'll take a look around in back. He is
out there, somewhere, in the back. (Two men
leave. Barbara goes to telephone)

MOTHER: (Weak but distinct) Thank you, all of you. What a
terrible pain it was. But it is better now. (Lies back
on sofa)

LAWYER: (Unpacking briefcase) I saved all the papers. Here
they are. Can we proceed?

MOTHER: Yes, we can. Listen to me. It was a test, a final test.
For me, it was the final birth pain of my oldest
child—(To Eric) That was nice of you, Eric. You
would defend me with the best you have, your
guitar. No part-time work this time, Eric. I am
very sorry, everybody, that it had to come to this.
But—I wanted to know, I had to be certain. No
test is ever as important as the final test—And
now—I am certain. Now I know. (Weaker) Bert,
how is your wound, does it hurt? Will it heal?

BERT: It is deep, and it hurts, but it will be okay—

MOTHER: Come closer, just a little. Your brother, Jack—I
never understood how two children could come
from the same womb and yet be so different—one
a hailstorm, and the other the gentle rain—My
mother, your grandmother, Bert, used to say to
me: take your two boys, put them into a large pot
and boil them for two hours—then let them start
life all over. My mother—bless her heart—

BERT: Don't strain yourself, Mother, please. (While he bends over sofa, Bess begins bandaging his arm)

MOTHER: Strain? No, there's no strain—no longer. The birth is—all over now. No more pain. (To Bert) And you, Mr. Ferryman, what advice do you have now? How do I get to the other shore? Can you tell me?

BERT: No, I can't. This journey, this final trip, if and when it comes, everybody has to take it—alone.

MOTHER: That's what I thought you would say. I have often thought about it, read about it, seen it in plays or movies—the last trip, those last steps, like your first, you must take them alone. There's no ferry-man, no pilot, not even a mother or father to hold your hand. (Everybody advances closer to the sofa) Except—that I don't believe it. I don't _want_ to believe it. It is true—all that traveling I did all over the world—I like it so much—except for the fact that I was always traveling alone. Bert, Bess, come closer, a little closer, please. 'All the world's a stage,' your brother quoted a little while ago, 'and all the men and women merely players... and one man in his time can play many parts..' When I'm gone, Bert, try to—become a ferryman of goods, for a while at least. Ferry goods. It is just as important as ferrying people. Heavier, at times. Take care of this world of mine, you and Bess, and of my people, these people—please.

(Two men enter noisily through back door)

FIRST MAN: The doctor is on his way.

CLERK: An ambulance is coming.

SECOND MAN: But there's no sign of that man, Jack Stone, no trace of him in the back, anywhere. He is gone. (Starts moving furniture, searching)

CLERK: Quiet, you two. Can't you see? Mrs. Stone, the proprietor, is very ill—

(Sudden absolute silence before curtain falls)

❧ ACT II ❧

Barbara Buttontrotter's apartment, one week later. When curtain rises, stage is dim and, on first appearances, resembles the General Store of Act I. As lights grow brighter, differences become clearer. Center stage is a living room with chairs, two sofas, table. Walls are covered with pictures, posters and assorted items from store: shells, skins, stuffed animals, etc. A spotlight should be playing on these for a while, then come to rest on Jack Stone. He's lying on one of the sofas, playing 'jacks' that he keeps throwing and catching in the air with dexterity. For a while, there is only the clacking noise of the game. Gradually, a second spotlight should separate from the first, go back over the walls and play on the various items, as before. This should go on for about 30 seconds.

Sudden hustle and commotion at apartment door. Someone is trying keys from the outside. Jack scoops up stones and quickly puts them into a pouch which he hides in his breast pocket. Soon Barbara enters. Jack gets up and goes toward her. He wears a long colorful robe.

JACK: (To Barbara, from behind her) Well, is it all over?
BARBARA: How you scared me just now, Jack. And why are

you wearing my robe? It was your mother's. She
—bequeathed it to me—years ago.

JACK: (Sweetly confidential) It makes me feel—
comfortable, dear. It makes me feel at home. But
tell me now: is it all over?

BARBARA: All over, except—the silence. The silence, then
the funeral, then the grave. What a day. (Sits down
and kicks off her shoes) What a day—what a party.
Just imagine—a wake—right inside our store—

JACK: It was Mother's idea—perhaps her greatest.
What imagination. I assume everybody was there?

BARBARA: (Quietly) No, not everybody. But many people
from the neighborhood. People you see perhaps
once a week, and talk to maybe once a year. One
of the garbage collectors came. He was recently
promoted to sanitation inspector, and he came to
check how may bottles were left. And St. Pierre,
the old blind man who used to sell pencils and
chestnuts at the corner. Well, he tottered in,
coughing and spitting blood. Said he had come
out of retirement for a day, just for Mother's wake.
And how they were all standing around and
talking—as if they knew her as their own mother.

JACK: Perhaps they did. Perhaps they did. (Walking the
floor) Mother had to be mother to somebody. If
her own boys wouldn't quite do, she'd adopt the
street and its people. (Sits down)

BARBARA: And many of them cried. Really cried—off and

on. Must have been the drinks—And of course
our store family was there. Eric and your
brother, Bert—

JACK: And his wife, Bess, she too?

BARBARA: No, Bert came alone this time. He said Bess
would come to the funeral, tomorrow. And after
the wake was over, it was he, Bert, who locked up
the store. Said he would come here, to my place,
after he had had a bite to eat.

JACK: (Melancholy) So, Bert came alone? Alone, like
myself. Except that I was here all day long. Locked
up. Alone. The panther in his cage dancing circles
around his own soul, as some poet said.

BARBARA: (Snappy) Cut the poetry, Jack, and consider
yourself lucky that you are not locked up some
where else, right now. The man you shot at the
airport—he is recovering, the newspapers say.
But his buddies are still out looking for you. Will
probably be looking for a long time—

JACK: (Pacing floor again) Everybody there, except me.
And I am the oldest. I suppose I could have
arrived at the store disguised as a street bum, with
brim hat and cane. It was always one of my
favorite roles, and I could still play it. (Puts on
appropriate items which he takes down from wall,
and playacts for a while) But—it's too late now,
anyhow. And they're not likely to look for me
here. Nobody knows about us two—(sharply)

unless you talked —

BARBARA: Me? Never. Not a word, even to Mrs. Stone. All these years—never a word. I always stuck to my man—Knopftraber. (Sharp laugh) But—why are you wearing my robe, Jack?

JACK: I told you. It makes me feel—secure. It was my mother's robe. Every son wants to wear his mother's robe, just once. Besides, I like it. Excellent material. Silk, right?

BARBARA: Yes. She brought it back from one of her trips around the world.

JACK: I like it. (Lies on sofa)

BARBARA: (Wistfully) I wish Lili could have been there, today. She always liked the store so much, and all those things in it, and Mrs. Stone. I wish she could have been there. Too bad—but she had to work and could not get time off.

JACK: She still in that restaurant?

BARBARA: On no, she works in a club now, a private club. Very exclusive, and very important work, she says. That's why they would not give her time off today. But she said over the telephone that she might come here later on tonight. Just for a while

JACK: (Sits up) Come here? Wait a minute. Didn't you just say my brother Bert was coming over, too? What are you up to again?

BARBARA: Me? Up to? Nothing, absolutely nothing. I just thought—Mr. Stein, your brother, after what

happened—he must be feeling alone, sort of—
and in this big city—And Lili can be such good
company, so cheerful—

JACK: (Grunts) What the hell are you up to?

BARBARA: (Pensive) She was always such an unusual girl,
our little Lili. Once, I remember, she called me in
the middle of the night, and I went into her
bedroom, and there she was, sitting on her bed—
"Mommy, Mommy," she whispered, "I just had
the most wonderful dream. I was Cinderella lying
on my bed in a deep sleep, and the handsome
prince came in and bent over me—"

JACK: (Rudely) Very unusual story. Very original. Why
do you bother to tell me?

BARBARA: (Confidentially) Because in her dream, the
prince did not kiss Lili—

JACK: No? (Plus short ad-lib remark)

BARBARA: (Undaunted) No. Instead, our Lili dreamt that
she got up, put her arms around the prince and
then kissed _him_—

JACK: Romantic trash, and reversed, yet. I must say—she
—and her dreams, and you and your schemes.
And damn you both
(Stomps feet on floor—childish)

BARBARA: (Unperturbed) But you haven't seen our Lili for
some time now. She has become quite a woman.
No Cinderella, her, no sugar princess. All woman
—woman.

JACK: (Nervous) But you are sure that neither she nor
my brother knows I am here—or about us? You
swear it?

BARBARA: (Solemnly) I swear it. I never breathed the
thought—to anyone. This is our secret, and it will
always be—

JACK: But what am I going to do whey they come here?

BARBARA: You can always go into the bedroom. You know
the way, I'm sure—

JACK: The hell I will. J'y suis, j'y reste (Sits down, grandly)

BARBARA: And whatever _that_ means. (Takes jacket and
sweater off) And whatever _you_ decide to do.
(Suddenly very hard) You _did_ say you were going
to pay me, right? You did say you had the
money, right?

JACK: (Nonchalantly) Of course, I did. Of course, I will.
I'll have the money as soon as I get it from the
jeweler. He kept some of the stones and he's
appraising them right now. And he will pay me as
soon as I can get out of this hole.

BARBARA: (Threatening) Stones—our stones—my stones
and your mother's stones. You know it was not
right to take them. And I'm telling you now: if I
don't get the money, these stones will turn into—
kidney stones—your kidney stones. You just wait
and see.

JACK: (Gesture) Look who is talking—Lady Virtue giving
us a lecture. You are crazy about this—my stones,

her stones, Mother's stones. Nobody owns stones, nobody except the earth. Us—we just take what we find—(Sudden ring of doorbell. Jack jumps up, grabs his shoes, clutches them to his chest, disappears through side door into bedroom, just as Lili, let in by Barbara, enters through main door. She is eloquently dressed in tight well-fitting clothes on an excellent figure. Accentuated sureness of walk and talk)

BARBARA: Oh, Lili, I'm so glad you could come over. Had a hard day at work, dear?

LILI: (Throws bag, gloves, jacket on sofa, sits down next to them) Not, too hard. Work likes ours is never really too hard. And my workday, on which the sun never shines, had not even begun yet.

BARBARA: What ways you have with words—so, you won't be able to stay very long today?

LILI: An hour, perhaps.—But where is everybody? You said on the phone others would be coming. Gentlemen, you said. Funny, when I came in I thought the place smelled a little like men.

BARBARA: They ARE coming, they ARE coming. Just sit with me, and wait a little while. Tell me, how's your job? Tell me all about it. (Both sit down at table. Barbara takes Lili's hand, but Lili gets up and begins to pace. Occasionally, to make a point, she strikes palm of her hand with gloves)

LILI: Oh, it's better than just being a waitress. Long

hours, though, very long. Most of the guests don't arrive until late, although some stay at the Club permanently, as residents. 'Lifers' we call them. They are pretty well adapted, and even considerate. The others—they just come and go, like birds pecking at a feeder.

BARBARA: And when do you get your sleep? When do you eat?

LILI: (More softly) Now you are talking like a mother to her child. (Changing to hard tone of voice) You could say that sleep—is part of my work. I eat whenever it is convenient. Sometimes with one of the guests, as a special treat. Usually a big brunch after we get up—before we start with the chores —like cleaning. (Sits down, continues in dream like mood) Most of all, I wish I did not have to wear the chains of work—my work. Unless they were of pure gold—my gold. I wish I could live like the snow goose—going north in the summer and south in the winter. Going, flying, but always knowing where I am going, and never going alone. (She gets up and reaches for her jacket. Doorbell rings, Barbara jumps up, opens door. Bert enters, looks around)

BARBARA: Oh, Mr. Stone—how nice—so nice you could come. And did you have a good meal somewhere on the way?

BERT: (Tired but precise; throughout the following scene

he will have to adapt his mood, speech, and
actions to various levels of evening energy) The
meal was all right. And the name is Stein,
Herbert Stein.

BARBARA: (Effusively warm, contrast to Lili's coldness) Of
course—and I'm sorry. I assure you it won't
happen again, Mr. Bert. (Looking around) Have
you met Lili? May I introduce my Lili?

BERT: (Tired, leaning back in chair) How do you do.

LILI: (Precise) How do you do. (They shake hands
formally, then take seats at opposite ends of table.
Bert draws up another chair and puts up his feet.
Lili watches)

BERT: God—what a day. What commotion, hustle. That
crowd—lively as reeds in a gale—around a live
coffin. No respect, I'm afraid, no respect. But
Mother would probably have liked it that way.
(Reaches into his pockets for pipe, tobacco)

BARBARA: She would, for sure, Mr. Stone. The day was
exactly as she would have wanted it. Air and
people—people. Isn't that so, Mr. Stone? By the
way, you probably don't remember my Lili. You
haven't seen her for so may years now, ever since
you moved to the city...

BERT: (Still searching for pipe, tobacco, etc.) No, I
wouldn't have known her. She certainly is no
longer Little Lili, as we used to call her...

BARBARA: (Leaning toward Bert; confidentially) Her name

isn't really Lili, you know...

BERT: (Absentminded) No, I didn't know that—Say—
you wouldn't have a little tobacco in this house,
would you?

BARBARA: (Stays in her place, while Lili, with sudden
laugh, gets up and looks into several drawers) Lili
is short for—how does it go?—Her father
thought it up—

LILI: (Turns around; sharply) For heaven's sake,
mother stop, will you—

BARBARA: Li—Li—what was it again? Can't
remember—Li —

LILI: Found it. Here. Couple of cigars. Will they do?

BARBARA: Li—Li—found it? Lili is short for 'Liebesleid'
(pronounces it carefully and correctly)

BERT: (Just as carefully) Lie-bes-leid.

BARBARA: (Busily) It has something to do with love—love
—something. I don't remember—

BERT: (Lights a cigar; heavy puffs) Love—pain, to
be precise—

LILI: (Turns to Bert, sharply. Repeats the word,
'Liebesleid', but mispronounces it: li-bes-leed)
'Libesleed'—you told me about that before,
Mother. But you said it was _your_ idea to give me
that crazy name. And now, you just pretend it was
my father's idea (Dreamily) Father, Father, who is
Father, anyhow? Li—li—li —ly—ly—ly Libes
leed—leeeed—(Takes a few dance steps)

BERT: Interesting, the way you are saying this
(Puffs on cigar)

LILI: Say what?

BERT: The way you pronounce your name, like:
li-bes-leed.

LILI: So what? I can't help it. I didn't give it to myself,
and I didn't take pronouncing in school In fact, I
never 'took' school, period. I got taken—out of it
—(Laugh) You—you're a schoolteacher, right?—

BERT: (While Barbara is making a frantic gesture trying
to interrupt Lili) At least, you know the difference
between 'took' and 'taken'. It's a start—So, now,
I'll tell you the difference between 'Liebesleid'
and 'libesleed' (Leibeslied)—

LILI: (Sits down, listens sullenly) So—tell me.

BERT: (Gets up; speaks clearly, almost pedantically)
'Love Pain' and 'Body Song.'

LILI: Body Song

BARBARA: (Gets up) I thinks I'll go into the next room and
change into something better. Excuse me, both of
you. I'll be back soon. (Goes into bedroom Jack
Stone had disappeared into before)

LILI: Body Song?

BERT: It's just what we call a literal translation. You
might say it's the rough shell of a good word that
was given a, sort of, bad name—

LILI: (Dreamily) Body song—love pain—

BERT: Leibeslied and Liebesleid—(Resolute) I'm sorry. I

didn't mean to—decline—I mean change your name. The translation just came to me, suddenly. Words always do—

LILI: (Interested) Oh, that's all right. I don't understand the meaning of the words completely, but I find them—appealing. They sound interesting. (Walks up and down the room, reciting the two words several times, eventually correctly) By the way, what's a 'translation'? Sounds like some kind of change—

BERT: (Disregarding the last question) Oh yes, it's interesting, all right. To me, at least. We used to speak German at home, you know. And later on, I taught German in high school, for a while.

LILI: And now—what do you do?

BERT: I am still teaching. But as I'm getting older I've thought about giving it up. Some day, I might do that—terrible thing, to sit around and wait for retirement age to come—(Last sentence said to himself) but—never mind—

LILI: You're still teaching—German—they call you libesleed, perhaps—

BERT: No, something that's called 'humanities'—it's a little bit of everything: language, art, history, science, music. It's interesting stuff. So much to learn—so much to teach, but even there, after a while you feel, you run out of fuel—

LILI: Oh—

BERT: And you? (Sits down beside her)

LILI: Oh—in a way, I teach, too. And some day, I too
        may want to change to something different—
        something better.

BERT: (Leans head back; now tired, naive) You? Teach?
        Where? What? (Suddenly alive, sitting up but
        acting almost stupidly) Then—we are—colleagues,
        in a way? (Music is heard coming from the
        bedroom, occasional noise, laughter, moving
        of chairs. Music gets gradually louder)

LILI: (Comfortable, superior laugh) Colleagues—
        another one of those words! No, I don't do the
        kind of teaching you do—and not in the kind of
        your place, professor—

BERT: (Puffing on cold cigar) In that club of yours,
        I suppose.

LILI: (Walks toward backstage) I wonder if mother has
        anything left to eat. I'm hungry. Nothing between
        my teeth since morning. (Raps rudely on bedroom
        door) Hey, Mom, anything to eat in this place?
        (Music stops abruptly)

BARBARA: (Opening door by a crack and shouting) Yeah,
        there's food in the fridge. Help yourselves, the
        two of you. (Sudden loud laugh from bedroom,
        two laughters blending into one. Music begins
        again. Lili recoils from door, goes to refrigerator,
        takes out cold meat, pickles, piece of cake. Takes
        food to table)

BERT: (Had been snoozing but is suddenly awake) Is your club far from here?

LILI: (Cuts piece of cake) No, not far. Walking distance. I often walk over in the afternoon. To see Mom. Want some cake? (She begins to eat, but only very small bites)

BERT: I see. (Reaches for piece of cake, but does not take it)

LILI: (Nibbling) Funny—you asking me if I teach.

BERT: (Finally takes small piece of cake) Why's that so funny?

LILI: (Same superior laugh, less loud) Because so many of our guests come to us to—learn..

BERT: Learn? About what?

LILI: About love—new love, new pleasures. (Takes pickle from jar and puts it in her mouth) New peace, maybe—(She giggles, music increases from bedroom. Voices and laughter)

BERT: And you—you teach all that? Love, pleasure, peace? Certainly, much more than teachers in their classroom—

LILI: We try. And most of our—pupils seem— satisfied. But of course, many of them we see only once or twice—not like real teachers who see their students every day. (Leans back, dreamily)

BERT: Every school day, more or less, until the semester changes, or the year ends. Or until students exchange their classes for what some call the

school of life. (Leans back—tired) Well,
whatever, they say about schools—a teacher is
still in a class of his own. Still—

LILI: (Interrupting) Have you taken a hotel room for
the night?

BERT: No, thanks. I don't need one, I—

LILI: Come with me to the club. We often have friends
in our rooms. Come with me—

BERT: You're nice to invite me, but—(Music and noises
from bedroom)

LILI: And many times we have guests who just come
drifting in like snow through the porch door. They
never even heard of the Club before... Then
suddenly, they change from cold to warm. They
melt—ice to soft water... (Gestures and
movements which Bert watches intently)
Sometimes, it makes me feel as if I am bathing a
baby—(Sudden loud noises from bedroom. Music
stops after radio crashes to floor. Steps)

BERT: (Jumps up and goes to bedroom door) What's
going on? Who's in there?

LILI: (Gets up, too, snatches piece of cold meat, puts it
into mouth) Let's get away from here. Let's go. I'm
going back to the Club. (Bert hesitates, half sits
down. Shouts from bedroom: 'no—no,' etc. Door
suddenly opens. Barbara appears, now wearing
Mrs. Stone's rob. More shouts of: 'no—no' no
more. Enough, enough. I want no more...)

Jack   (Running after Barbara) Stay here, you bitch. And give me back my mother's robe. Now.

BERT: (Confused) Jack? You here? (Tries to step between Jack and Barbara)

JACK: (Pushes him back) Leave us alone, and get out of my way. And get her back in that room. (Scuffle between Jack and Bert)

BARBARA: No, no. Not again. Not for you. (Steps around Bert and behind Jack whom she drags backwards into a chair while Jack and Bert are still scuffling. Jack falls back into chair. Lili jumps into his lap. Jack cries out. Brief struggle. Jack slumps back, Lili gets up quickly)

BERT: (Confused) Jack—you been here all the time?

BARBARA: He's been here for a week now, ever since he— got away from the store. You remember, don't you, Mr. Bert?

BERT: Yes, I remember now, I remember well. (To Jack) And the police have been after you all the time. _You_ remember that, don't you?

JACK: (From chair, sharply) Yes, I do. I know it. But— they can't look everywhere. And if you—any of you—say a word about where I am—we'll all have to pay the price. I for what I did—and Barbara for giving me shelter. And that wouldn't be exactly what Mother ordered, would it, Bert?

LILI: (Worried) I'm going back to my Club. Back to work. (Replaces food. To Bert) Coming?

BERT: I'll go with you as far as your club, yes. But then, I'm going on to the store. I'll spend the night there. (Lili laughs as Bert takes her arm and the two exit. Jack and Barbara close door behind them, then shake hands spontaneously and go back toward bedroom as curtain falls)

❧ ACT III, SCENE 1 ❧

The following morning. Same scene as ACT I., but store sign has been changed to THE STONE BOX. In center stage stands a large, plain wooden coffin. In front of it stands sofa from which Bert rises shortly after curtain has gone up. Lights, first dim, get gradually brighter. Speaking, during entire scene, very precise, but always in hushed tone of voice.

BERT: (Fumbling around for shoes, coat, tie, etc.) Seven-thirty. Time to to get up. Strange night, but I slept well—considering the choices I had—Lili's club, our hotel—(Gets off sofa, goes briefly behind coffin where he bends down as if he were touching or checking something, then returns to front stage where he makes efforts to comb hair, get dressed, etc.) Time—funny thing how it gets into your bloodstream. Just like the food we eat. I swear it—there won't be a day for the rest of my life when I won't wake up by at least seven-thirty. Just because I've always done it. Oh yeah, I know: 'Early to bed, and early to rise...' I know—that's what I'm paid for: to know. But in the guts I know differently—slavery—that's what it is—the

slavery of habit. (Sits down, puts on one shoe)
Should have become a monk. Then you make the
habit your life—simple—no more slavery—
(Goes behind coffin once more. Same action.) For
the night. What for? To extend life, after death? To
snatch another twelve hours from the depth of
days and nights, lost in the business of shells and
skins and trinkets? Foolish of you, Mother, too—
to have the funeral delayed for a week, to have
decided to spend your last night in the store.
(Addresses coffin) But never mind—and excuse
me—de mortuis nihil nisi bene—only good
things said about the dead. Wonder what gave
you the idea, though. Your life, of course. Your
death is your life—(Reaches for his coat and in
getting up knocks over a chair. Noise) Hey,
Professor, easy there. You're still drugged by your
sleep, man. Easy there. We'll have enough noise
when the undertakers come and take you out of
your store—for good. You, in there, your travels
all over now—except for the final trip, in your
wheel-less coach in your wooden box. How much
time have we left? Two hours and a half. How
much time can weigh once you put it on a scale.
Like water—it runs and it weights—I still cannot
understand why I slept so well. Is this the way
you feel when you wake up from death, Mother?
Is this your first step toward eternity? And

afterwards? More steps? An endless number of them? Or—no steps at all? And no more time? Eternity—the perfect time—no time at all—like the perfect government—no government at all— Hold it, Professor. No class today (Sharp knocks on front door. Bert jumps off sofa, one shoe on, one off. Stops for second to glance at coffin behind him. Another loud knock) All right, all right. Coming, coming. Take it easy, whoever you are, or you'll waken us all. (He unlocks front door and immediately puts his finger on his lips asking for quiet. Enter lawyer. Dark suit, stiff hat, briefcase, pompous)

LAWYER: (Briskly) Good morning, Mr. Stein. (Bert keeps finger on his lips. Lawyer lowers his voice) I see you're already here. Is everything all right?

BERT: Certainly—what did you think?

LAWYER: I think what I see. (Takes brief look around front part of store. Then sits down at table not far from sofa) And what I see is—that everything is as ordered in the will. Provided that box still contains . . .

BERT: Let's not be brutal, Drossel. Of course, it does. What did you expect? Grave robbers? Necromancers? You need not have bothered coming here so early in the morning!

LAWYER: True—I could have just called you. But I had to come anyhow—so, what's a few hours earlier? In

this kind of situation? And in any case,
I had to come—

BERT: Had to come? Why?

LAWYER: Why? Don't you know? Didn't you get the
message? I had to go to the airport and pick up
your wife, Bess. She flew in, early.

BERT: (Gets up roughly, knocks over chair again) Bess?
She's in town? Coming here? With you? And how
did _you_ know she was coming?

LAWYER: (With dignity) She telephoned my office last
night. Tried to reach you, too, but could not. Said
she would send you a telegram. Didn't you get it
—at the hotel? Did you check the front door?
(Knocks and commotion on side door) That
would be she, right now. She wanted to stop at the
store to get a few things for breakfast.

BERT: (Hurried talk and actions. Puts on jacket, slips into
second shoe) Tell you what—let's all go out for
breakfast together. There's a good diner a few
doors down the street. Open early. Pat and Jim's
—excellent food—(Rushes toward side door,
pulling Lawyer along, taking in hushed but
urgent tone of voice. Lawyer struggles but doesn't
really resist. Bert opens door just as Bess enters,
bag of groceries in her arm)

BESS: (Cheerful but subdued) Oh—there you are, Bert.
Good morning. I See you got here early. (Puts bags
on table in front stage)

BERT: (Nervous, tying shoelace) And so did you. Had a good flight? But—you might a least have let me know you were coming...

BESS: I tried, but there was no answer in the hotel room. Didn't you get my telegram, either? (Walks to front door which she unlocks)

BERT: No I didn't. And I was just suggesting to Mr. Drossel we should all go out together for breakfast...

BESS: Go out? Not necessary. I just bought a few things. We'll eat here— let me just—I know where the kitchen is—(She starts in direction of backstage, but Bert tries to block her way)

BERT: (Urgent) Bess. I am asking you and Mr. Drossel to go out for breakfast—please—I have my reasons—I want to get out of here. This is a morgue—not a place for eating, not today—

BESS: What is with you, Bert? You sound as if you are in such a hurry—as if you spent the whole night here—

BERT: I did.

BESS: (Snappy) You did—and alone, I hope. (Puts hand over her mouth) Of course not, forgive me, please. I didn't mean it that way. I am still tired from the long flight. Of course, we'll go out for breakfast, if you want to. Let me just put these groceries away, and then we'll go. If you wouldn't mind, Mr. Drossel... (She picks up grocery bags, then turns

and walks toward backstage, and just as she
passes the coffin she stops, lets out soft scream,
drops groceries, as from behind coffin rises,
stretching both arms upward.

LILI: Wait for me, everybody. My god, what a racket
you are all making—so early in the morning. You
aren't going to leave me alone—here?
(Commotion. Bess tries to pick up groceries.
Lawyer grunts. Bert tries to push Lili down)

LAWYER: What is this? Who are you? Why are you here?
Where did you come from? Speak up, please.

BERT: (Sits down, puts head in hand) Her name is Lili.

BESS: (Composed) Lili—of course, Lili Traber.
Barbara's girl.

LAWYER: (Persisting) What are you doing here, young lady?

BERT: She spent the night here.

BESS AND LAWYER: With you?

BERT: Let me explain.

LAWYER: Incredible. (To Lili) Young lady, I think, first of all,
you ought to get dressed.

LILI: I will, I will. Just give me time to wake up. God—
what a night. What a place to sleep. I must have
been out of mind to come here last night instead of
going back to the Club. But strangely enough—I
slept well until you woke me up just now. Right
next to the coffin—I slept well, like a dead person
myself. (Modestly) Excuse me, gentlemen. But I'll
just get myself back into shape and form. It won't

take me long. (Gets up and drowsily walks toward back of store from which Bess is just returning. Looks are exchanged, but no words)

BESS: Yes, Bert. I guess you had better explain to us what happened. Mr. Drossel, could you stay a little while longer, please? The coffee will be ready in no time...

BERT: (Sits down, searches pockets for pipe and lighter) We met last night, at Mrs. Buttontrotter's, apartment. She had invited me to come up and—relax, I guess, after the long day here at the store. I went, but only for a short while, before going to the hotel—

BESS: Yes?

BERT: But then, there was this girl, this—Lili. I had not seen her for years. And suddenly there she was a grown woman now...

LAWYER: Quite so—

BERT: (Warming up, lighting his pipe) So—we talked about what has happened—Mother's death, you know—and ...

BESS: And?

BERT: And her name—especially her name. Did you know that her name, Lili, was only an abbreviation?

BESS: No, I didn't know that.

BERT: An abbreviation for 'Liebesleid'—love pain.

BESS: (Cool) You've always had a hound's nose for sniffing out unusual words—

LAWYER: (Mispronounces) Libesleed—interesting sounds—
(Short burst of song backstage)

BESS: And what else? Was there anything else last night?
'Liebesleid?' (correct pronunciation)

BERT: Yes—Mrs. Buttontrotter and—(Quick glance in
direction of backstage) and eventually, shortly
before midnight, I decided to go back to the hotel,
and Lili to her club. And as we were walking
along the street, she became increasingly
depressed. Said she didn't want to go back to the
Club anymore, said she didn't want to go back to
work, just rest and sleep. So—knowing we still
had two sofas in the store, I brought her back here,
and she spent the night back there—behind
Mother's coffin—

BESS: And that's all?

BERT: That's all. (Lawyer gulps, Bess shrugs, shakes
head, opens hands in indifferent gesture)

BESS: Well, I hear the coffee stopped perking. Let's all
have breakfast. (Goes quickly backstage, returns
with coffee pot, cups. While Bess pours coffee, Lili
returns from other side of backstage, sits down at
table, is given coffee and begins to speak, dreamily)

LILI: I felt last night—that sleep must be an oracle of
death—the oracle that speaks—confused and
hidden by a cloud of vapor—rising behind rocks
—like morning mist from streets—(All have
suddenly stopped drinking and eating, all listen

to Lili. Just as she is about to speak again, there is another commotion at front door. Enter Barbara followed by an old man whom she half drags half pushes through the door)

BARBARA: (Cheerfully) Good morning, everybody—Lili, Mr. Bert, Mrs. Stone—

BESS: Stein—

BARBARA: A very sad day for all of us, indeed, but we must not be gloomy. Eric called me early this morning. He has a job for today, so he won't be here for the final ceremonies. So instead I brought along old St. Pierre. You all know St. Pierre, of course don't you? He usually sells chestnuts at the corner. I passed him on my way here, just now and he wanted to know what has happened to Mrs. Stone. When I told him about her death, he began crying, poor man. Then he asked me if he could come to the funeral. He was very fond of Mrs. Stone, you see, so I brought him along. Poor old man—since his illness he can barely hear or see. Sit down, St. Pierre, and I'll pour you some coffee. (She puts the old man down in a chair, then goes backstage. On her way, she looks at the two sofas and the coffin. Shrugs her shoulders. St. Pierre, wrapped in a knitted scarf and wearing big dark glass, keeps shaking hands and knees after sitting down. Says nothing)

LAWYER: I remember him—the name is Jules St. Pierre—

right—although until recently I never knew he had a name. I remember how he used to stand at the corner with his cart and coal fire. On a cold night, I used to buy a bagful of chestnuts from him. Good stuff on cold November nights. But— I remember reading in the papers that he died a few weeks ago—they even had a funny little headline: 'Jules St. Pierre—a Fixture Falls'—or some thing like that—I'm a little mixed up on this —anyhow —

BARBARA: (Returns with more coffee from backstage and cuts into lawyer's speech) No, he wasn't dead, just ill, very ill. Had to stay in bed for weeks. And now he is back, and here he is, such as he is —And here we are, all of us. (Sits down on armrest of St. Pierre's chair. He makes a weak sign as if he wanted to say something, but is kept silent by Barbara with strong stab of her elbow. St. Pierre slumps back in chair, slurps coffee)

LILI: (Still speaking in a kind of trance, stirring her coffee, oblivious of what has just been said) The mist changed into dew—and change was all around me, and all inside—no longer was I Lili— Lili Liebesleid lay in a coffin next to Mrs. Stone's —

BARBARA: (Pretends to choke on coffee, produces a sharp hissing sound: 'Shsh—Shsh') She—sh—(Bess silences her with strong gesture)

LILI: We change—overnight—young fillies into
mares—and virgin into vermin—Yet, there I
slept—and in the sleep of death found beauty,
peace, forgiveness—the love of Mother's death
—(St. Pierre slurps down last swallow of coffee.
Lawyer clatters his cup noisily)

LAWYER: (Gruffly) Well—should we complete the legal
business before the undertaker's men arrive? We
have a little time—just a little—

BERT: Good idea. Even though this hardly seems the
place for business—(St. Pierre slams cup into
saucer, slumps back in chair)

BARBARA: This place has always been business—

LAWYER: Very well then. (Opens his briefcase) Here is the
accounting: the testament of Mrs. Stone... (Reads
in stolid, professional manner) Last will and
testament... rendering invalid, etc., etc...

BERT: The entire text, if you please...

LAWYER: Rending invalid all my previous wills... And now
to the point: 'Whichever of my two sons Jack and
Bert, will be present in my store on the day of my
funeral and shall be able and willing to sign the
attached _Declaration of Responsibility_, he shall be
heir to my store and fortune providing he also be
willing and able to take care of my employees:
Barbara Buttontrotter, full-time employee, and
Eric Traber, part-time employee. In the case that
both sons shall be present on said day and said

occasion, the older one, Mr. Jack Stone, presently
of no certain address, shall be the heir, provided
he be willing to sign said _Declaration_ (Lawyer gets
up from chair and looks around from person to
person) I see her Mr. Herbert Stein, present on the
day of Mrs. Stone's funeral. Mr. Herbert Stein, are
you willing and able to sign this _Declaration_? (Bert
gets up, looks around the store, then at all those
present. He looks back at the coffin, then for a few
seconds at St. Pierre, who is stirring his empty cup
with his spoon. Finally, he looks at his wife, Bess,
who simply nods)

BERT: I am ready to sign. Could you hand me the papers,
please?

LILI: (Firmly but polite) One moment please, Mr. Stein.

BERT AND BESS: (After shore pause) Yes...?

LILI: (Slowly but very clearly) Would you consider me
—a part of this world—this big box that will
come to a new life? May I become —a branch of
this new tree?

BERT: (Signs papers without paying attention to Lili.
Hands papers back to Lawyer) Here you are, Mr.
Drossel. I have signed the _Declaration_.

LILI: (Calmly) May I?

BESS: Why?

LILI: To learn...

BERT: What could you learn that you don't already
know?

LILI: To live...

BERT: We might try it out for a while. We might try to learn and—live— from each other in this small world. Oneself—and the knowledge of oneself—these are things that we can truly share. (Suddenly decisive, very cordial to Lili) Yes, Lili, there will be a place for you here, in this new, small world. (Sharp knock on front door. St. Pierre drops cup to floor. Barbara gives him another stab with her elbow)

LILI: (With sincere enthusiasm) Thank you, thank you, Mr. Stein. You won't be sorry—I swear it—you won't be sorry for what you just said. (back to her dream-like speech) In one of my dreams last night I heard my mother scream at my dad—chasing him out of the bedroom. But all he wanted was to wear his mother's robe, his mother's robe— (Silence for a second, then more knocks at front door. Lawyer gets up and opens door)

VOICES: We are from Dunne's Mortuary, sir. Is everything ready for the funeral? (All get up and stand around coffin, except for St. Pierre who gets down on his knees and gropes for pieces of his broken cup. Curtain)

⋈ ACT III, SCENE 2 ⋈

A morning, one month later. As curtain opens, Lili and Eric are seen to be busy hanging modern wall posters, and arranging others for display on a long counter on left side of stage. Bess and Barbara are leaning over similar counter on right side of stage, watching activities on left counter. St. Pierre sits on floor near right counter. Entire act goes on very lively, but with occasional intermittent breaks of complete silence.

LILI: Help me with these posters, Eric. They must go up higher. (She climbs on stool or small step ladder. Modest dress, slacks or plain skirt)

ERIC: (Without emotion) Yes, sister. (Climbs up after Lili and helps) Will this be high enough?

LILI: Yes, thank you. But—please—stop calling me sister. Please.

BARBARA: (Stands up and shouts) Yes, stop calling her sister.

ERIC: Why? (Jumps to floor) It's true, isn't it?

BARBARA: The truth has nothing to do with it.

ERIC: The truth is the truth, and it always has something to do with everything. My truth with me—yours with you—ours with us. Besides, if Lili goes

along the way she has these past few weeks, she
will not only be my sister, but a sister—period.

BARBARA: (Calmer, speaking first to herself) Half sister, at
best. (To Eric) What do you mean?

ERIC: She is so different now. She no longer seems—a
woman. She's a girl—again. She has changed.
She is acting—almost like a sister.

BARBARA: You mean a nun?

BESS: (Closes a drawer sharply. Loud voice) Hah—that
would be the day. Our Lili a nun. And who would
she be? Sister Lili? Sister Liebesleid? Sister
Leibeslied?

LILI: (Still on top of stool or ladder) There—isn't it
beautiful? Love is—a mouthful of joy.

BESS: Beautiful kitsch—and I hope it sells.

BARBARA: What? Love? Joy? A mouthful? (Moment of
silence, then Eric begins to hum)

ERIC: Haven't done too well with the skin and the shell.
(Takes up guitar, strums a few chords. Bert enters
briskly through side door)

BERT: Good news, everybody. The bank has approved
the loan. Just signed the final application form.
Here! (Waves papers) Business improvement loan.
We'll renovate the entire store, buy new
merchandise, branch out—(Looks around and
waves briskly at everybody. St. Pierre gives slight
stir as papers are waved in his direction) I see we
have been busy again. Good work, Lili. I like that

poster: Love is a mouthful—

BESS: (Sternly) It's trashy, but I'll like it if it sells.

ERIC: I like it as it is. It—sings. (He plays a few more chords trying make up a tune for 'Love is...)

BARBARA: Mouthful or not—as I have been saying these last weeks: I am ready for business right now. Come on, customers. Come in, folks. No more wakes in here now, no more coffins. Business as usual.

BERT: Just wait until we complete our renovation. You'll see how this place comes alive—

BARBARA: And we are going to sell shells, as we did before. As Mrs. Stone used to say: things go well, shell by shell. Said she learned it from her late husband who, in turn, had learned it in the war—only a little different: things go to hell, shell by shell...

LILI: (Firmly) I think that renovation is better than past habits. I agree with Mr. Bert. Let's all work together. Let's all help out, and each other. There'll be strength in our group...

ERIC: And harmony in our combo... (Bert has listed to Lili with obvious pleasure. He now puts out his hand to help her come down the ladder. Lili jumps down by herself)

BESS: I think I'll order more hats. Hats sell in spring. Later we'll have more skins, for fall and winter... (St. Pierre stirs, draws his hat deeper over his face, pulls collar of his coat around his neck, mumbles while others are silent)

ST. PIERRE: Spring hats and fall skins. Spring hats and fall
skins. (He rolls over and pretends to sleep)

BERT: (To Eric and Lili) You agree with me then.
Renovation. (Reaches for Lili's hand, but she with-
draws) You're right, Eric. Harmony will be the
thing. We could play together—trio, quintet—

ERIC: (Quietly) Just a simple combo. Maybe we could
also start a record department. Here, I just picked
up the latest hits. (He takes several records from
counter, also a small record player which he plugs
into outlet. He puts on a record but hesitates to
start playing)

BARBARA: (Confused first, but soon determined) And I
have still another. Here, St. Pierre (pulls St. P to
his feet), stand outside the front door for a while.
Display some of our items. Take some of these
shells, put them into a basket. There—I bet this
will attract attention. Up, on your feet now. (She
pulls him to his feet and tries to steer him toward
the door. He shakes himself loose, walks to one of
the counters, reaches into his coat pocket and
takes out stones. Begins playing 'jacks'. All look on.)

ERIC: I think I'll go out too and rearrange our display
case. Another little renovation. Be back soon. (To
St. P) Coming? (He takes St. P by the arm and both
leave through front door)

BERT: (Opens drawers in left counter) Where did I put

our other sample posters, yesterday? Oh, here
they are. Lili, will you help me pick the best...(Sits
on top of counter. Lili jumps up and sits next to
him. Together, they unroll several posters)

BARBARA: Cozy scene. (To Bess) Wish we could do this too,
together. Want to try?

BESS: Yes, especially with all these spiny shells on the
counter. After you, Buttontrotter. (Gesture)

BARBARA: (Jumps up on counter too, deftly landing right
next to one of the shells) How about some music?
And some news on the radio, to pass the time?
(Reaches up to radio and turns it on. Just then,
Eric and St. P come back through front door. Eric
lies down on sofa standing between counters in
center backstage)

LILI: (Elaborately affected speech. Reads from one of
the posters) Love and desire...

BERT: (Reads from same poster)... are the spirit's wings...

ERIC: Y-a-a-a. (Spreads out arms and legs and raises
them toward ceiling)

LILI: Love and desire are the spirit's wings...

BERT: ...toward great deeds...

RADIO: (Barbara says some of it) Take Grippine every
hour, and free the world from colds...

BESS: (Puts another shell on counter) This too shall be
broken...

ERIC: (Still in same position) Y-a-a-a. (For a few seconds,
there is confusion of sounds and words. Each

actor ad-libs, as words happens to come to him)

BARBARA: (Turns radio up) Youth is in the news today.

RADIO: ... and smacked his bottom repeatedly with her
electric riding crop...

BARBARA: ...and smacked his bottom...

ERIC: (flapping arms and legs) Y-a-a-a.

BERT: Who? Us?—Just testing, testing...

RADIO: ...then hanged herself with an extension cord...

BARBARA: ... extension cord...

LILI: (Reading from another poster) Trust everybody,
but always roll your own dice... (St. Pierre is
standing behind right counter, plays 'jacks'
with stones)

BERT: Trust—you can trust me now, Lili, just as I
trust you—

LILI: (Jumps off counter. Shouts) What did you say?

BESS: Turn it off. Turn that radio off. (Covers her ears
with both hands)

BERT: (Shouts) Trust—

BARBARA: (Moves toward front door) Everybody—where
is everybody? Come and buy my skins
and shells...

LILI: (Climbs to top of stool or ladder) Did you want
cards, Mr. Bert? Did you want your future told?

BERT: Lili, cut it out. Lili—

BESS: Barbara, cut down that volume. (Barbara waltzes
over to radio,but turns volume up instead of down)

ERIC: (Gets up slowly from sofa, as if in a trance. Pulls

cord out of of wall socket—silence, absolute for a few seconds, while Eric tiptoes to his guitar which he picks up. Plays some flamenco) Dance—anybody? (While he plays, other actors begin jerky movements, almost like a dance but uneven. After about 10 seconds, St. Pierre steps from behind counter into center stage)

ST. PIERRE: (Happy and loud) A dance, a dance. (Sings with familiar tune) Standing at the front door, holding all the world, holding all the world in hand... But now, a dance for the world. (Barbara reconnects radio. Loud modern music. St. P. begins a slow crazy dance in center stage. As tempo increases, he takes off his sunglasses, hat, coat, scarf until gradually the person of Jack Stone emerges) Ha-ha-ha. It's me once again. The prodigal son is home again. The act has ended and the dream begins anew. Truth will prevail—truth and youth. Truth and youth.

LILI: (Jumps from ladder to counter, from there into Jack's arms. For a short time, they dance wildly. Side door is suddenly pushed open. Jack quickly scoops up his clothes and dives under right counter. The other actors continue their jerks for a second. Nobody comes through door. Barbara unplugs radio)

ERIC: You did that well, old man. Dance a little more for us. Nobody came in—just the wind, playing tricks with the door...

BARBARA: Don't speak to him like that. He could be your
—dad.

ERIC: But he isn't? Or is he?

BARBARA: (Lies down on sofa) No, he is not. Your father—
I never knew him, and he knew me just once. But
I knew his name: Knopftraber, Hans Knopftraber.
Oh Hans, Hans—(Bert and Lili lean over left
counter, Bess and St. Pierre over right counter.
Bert puts arm around Lili, and she does not with-
draw. All are watching Barbara's little scene)

ERIC: (Sitting on back of sofa) But—how did you know
his name?

BARBARA: His name? His name? (Continues to move about
sofa, speaking as if in a dream) He wrote me a
letter, just once. It had a little money in it. Came
from Africa, Ivory Coast, Africa—and that was
the time when Mrs. Stone decided to import
seashells. Oh Hans, Hans—

ERIC: (Loud) Knopftraber

BESS: (Louder) Buttontrotter

BERT: (Louder) Welttraber

ST. PIERRE: (Louder) World Trotter. (All shouting these
words at each other for a few seconds. There is no
definite plan or purpose. Then front door opens.
Enter Lawyer with same briefcase. St. Pierre dives
under counter, then reappears in his old
mascarade. Barbara gets off sofa and takes her old

place behind right counter. Lawyer sits down on sofa. Four-name shouting continues. Eric suddenly leaps from sofa to left counter)

ERIC: Music. Let's have more music with our words. (Puts noisy modern record on phonograph)

LILI: No, Eric. Not this noise, please. You play your guitar instead.

ERIC: (Shouts) What did you say? More music? Louder? Here—(Turns volume up)

BARBARA: (Stands up on right counter, steps on shells) Here—I can match this noise. (Turns radio on)

BESS: Stop it, Buttontrotter. Turn that radio off.

BARBARA: (Mimics) Leibeslied, Leibeslied.

BERT: Leibeslied, Leibeslied.

ST. PIERRE: (Comes up from under counter. Dances as before. Sings) Ferryman, ferryman, ist das nicht ein Ferryman. (He suddenly sees Lawyer. Stops his dance and hides under counter)

LILI: (Screaming) Father, Father? (All begin once more same jerky movements. Several seconds of noise and commotion. Lawyer who has been examining his papers suddenly puts them back in his brief case, turns off stereo and radio. Total silence. The counter groups stand still, then in unison they bend forward and look at Lawyer with hostility)

LAWYER: (Loud strict voice. Courtroom manners) If noise were your business, you would all be million-aires... As it is, your business, ever since Mrs.

Stone's death, has been—silent. (Takes papers out of briefcase) For a month now—losses, nothing but losses.

BESS: We are trying—

LILI: (To Lawyer) What business is it of yours, anyhow?

LAWYER:(Pompous) Your business is my business.

ERIC: (Loud strums on guitar) How's that?

LAWYER: Just a little clause in Mrs. Stone's will. I am to receive 20 percent of the store's profit for as long as I live. A dividend, so to speak. A kind of pension.

ST. PIERRE: (Jumps up from under counter) You crook! (Throws costume off, straightens up)

LILI: Father, Father! No, not now, not that!

LAWYER: (Stands up and shouts) Father? What? You? Mr. Stone? Jack Stone? Right here? The fugitive?

BARBARA: (Grandly) Yes—right here. Lili's father and here he will stay—and play his part of the young old man—until the tidal wave of indignant reproach has blown the beach full of seashells—and then carried itself back to the bottom of ocean.

ERIC: (More strong strums on guitar) Lili's father, but not mine—

BARBARA:(Coldly) No, not yours. You are Knopftraber's son. You will always be a Knopftraber.

LAWYER: I am—I am going to have this man arrested by the police, right now. I am going—

ERIC: (Blocks his way) Easy, man—and ruin our store —with your 20 percent profit? (Lawyer stops, then returns to sofa, sits down, down, opens brief case. Papers scatter. He bends down to pick them up. Other actors bend over their counters and once more begin their jerky movements. Phono and radio are again turned on. Eric plays guitar. St. Pierre and Lawyer turn up volume of radio and stereo. For a short while, there will be continuous noise made by music and random words and phrases that actors repeat from the play. Eventually, Lawyer will lie on sofa and cover his head with his briefcase. Jack will dance. Bert puts his arm around Lili. Bess throws shell at the two, but misses them. They embrace. Noise will rise to unbearable level. Suddenly, it stops. All motion on stage stops. Lights dim and out. Short pause in complete darkness. Long audible sigh. Curtain)

❧ Act III, Scene 3 ❧

The store, about six weeks later. The remodeling has been completed. There are modern wood and steel shelves The two sofas have been moved from center stage. There are new, modern lights. The old sign: STONE'S GENERAL STORE has been replaced above the main door. As curtain opens, Barbara is busy unpacking big box of shells. She hums and talks to herself.

CLERK: How nice it is to have things back in order—I mean, business is running on an even keel more or less. Not that I don't like a little excitement every now and then, but too much commotion, too much change—it makes you sick. Can't say that I like these new shelves, either. Too clean, too fine. But our old store sign is back. I knew it would be. Brought many of the old customers back, too, together with several new ones... Ah, yes, a new life it is on the old island—(She puts shells on new shelves. Soon front door is opened, chimes play first bars of a well-known tune.
Enter Customer 1)

CUST 1: (Dressed in a worn soldier's coat with rows of faded decorations. Military cap. Gloves. He looks

around for a few seconds, then speaks to Clerk)
You the General? General Store?

CLERK: Yes, I am—and here is one of my ammunition
boxes, just to prove my rank—and just in case.

CUST 1: Glad to have found you, General, and see you
once more. Used to serve under you—in Africa,
many years ago that was—and you looked
different then. You have—altered.

CLERK: We all have. You, too. But I think I remember you.
Yes, I think, I remember—

CUST 1: (Military salute) At your orders, General. I'm
happy you remember, and if you don't recall the
name, just call me soldier. That's what I was and
still am—the old soldier, forever marching, for
ever living in the service, refighting his battles, his
wars—winning some and losing others. You
selling guns too, with them shells, General?

CLERK: No, no guns. But we have that sword on the wall
behind you. (Walks over and takes sword off
hook) Here, want to see it? Want to hold it? A
beautiful weapon—and just 149.50. Want to buy
it? (Cust 1 unsheathes sword, puts it over his
shoulder, begins marching around. Just as he
passes side door, it opens in his face. Noise. Bert
enters carrying another big box)

BERT: This man—(Puts box on counter)

CLERK: Just a customer—and an old friend.

BERT: He—bothering you—dear—

CLERK: No, dear, not at all, dear. And if he did—I'd know
how to take care of him, wouldn't I?
(Confidentially) Especially now that I have been
promoted to general...

BESS: (Storms in through side door, very excited) I am
sick of it, sick and tired of it—

BERT: Of what, dear?

BESS: Of your 'dear'—Oh yes, I heard the two of you
talking. I heard it all. My ears are excellent. Dear
this, dear that—I'm just sick of it, you
understand. (She storms into center stage, runs
directly into Cust 1)

CUST 1: Aha—a body, at last, flesh and blood, the enemy,
perhaps. Take care, enemy. Maybe the old soldier
is not too old for a personal encounter. (He lowers
his sword at Bess who has suddenly become very
cool. She folds her arms over her chest and just
stand staring at Cust 1. Gradually, his sword sinks
lower and lower until it touches the floor) It's no
use—I knew it—I'm just too old for sword and
guns and shells. Sorry, General...

BESS: (Exaggerated laugh) Did you hear that, all of you?
Did you see that—an old soldier no longer able to
use his sword—why this is funny. Right, Bert?

BERT: Yes, dear. (Goes to Clerk's box and helps
her unpack)

CUST 1: Lady—whoever you are and whatever—don't
ever laugh at an old soldier—ever. Many years

THE ACCOUNTING

ago, he carried man's burdens with him into
battle—man's hatred, his killer lust, his ugly
moods, and much more—he carried all that into
battle. Fought, and in fighting lost his humanity,
lost himself. And since then, he is roving the earth
to seek and find what he lost. In vain, it's gone forever. But look he must and I know, it makes him
look strange and act even stranger. But—laugh
you must not. Please don't laugh at him. Sounds
of laughter can hurt more than bullet wounds—
Please, General, you tell them too: don't laugh—

CLERK: (Speaking to all) All right. You heard him—so
don't laugh anymore—And you, soldier, time
for you to get back into line—forward, march—
back into the battle of life. (Cust 1 marches out
through front door. All follow with their eyes)

BERT: Poor guy—he'll go on searching, but probably
not for the happiness promised in the
Constitution. He'll march on in search of himself,
but if he finds that, what will he have found?
What will he do?

CLERK: Oh, stop all this philosophy. Life goes on. Business
goes on. Help me unpack this box, will you, dear?

BESS: And there you go again with your 'dear.' Dear me
—it drives me up the wall. So stop it, the two of
you. Hear—

CLERK: Okay, okay—for heaven's sake, you—(Front
door opens. Chimes Enter Customer 2)

238

CUST 2: Good afternoon. (Everybody looks up. Cust 2 is a
woman in expensive almost stately dress, firm
straight bearing. In overall appearance she shows
a striking resemblance to the deceased Mrs. Stone.
As soon as she turns and looks at Clerk, there is a
loud shriek and crash as Clerk drops handful of
shells) Good afternoon, everybody. Did I startle
you? I am sorry if I did. Please forgive me. I heard
from friends that you had unusual items on
display in your store. May I see them, please? I so
like the distinct, individual, unusual—

CLERK: My word, how you resemble her. You could be—
her twin sister—or perhaps herself, come back to
the living—

CUST 2: Resemble? Whom?

BERT: Mrs. Stone, the late Mrs. Stone, my mother—

CUST 2: Twin sister? Resemble her? Mrs. Stone? My name,
for your information is Mrs. Vanderhusen, Gloria
Vanderhusen. And I have always thought of
myself as unique. Twin sister, indeed—

BESS: (Matter of fact) Until now.

CUST 2: Yes, I thought so, until now. But it seems I have
become a type, a sort of mirror image of a
certain—Mrs. Stone, you said? Stone—the
other side of a stone, perhaps? Its other face? (Sits
down) Funny coincidence. Just the other day a
child in the street, an urchin, shouted after me:
'hey you, hey you, stone-face, stone-face.' Is this

what I am? I, the wandering stone? The
peripatetic traveler who knows all the gold and
diamond spots? I? The wandering stone? (Looks
at herself in a mirror) Stone-face, stone-face—and
I had to come to this store, of all places, to find out

BERT: So did I—

CUST 2: But did you, really? Find out?

BERT: I'm not sure. I think perhaps I did.

CUST 2: As for myself, I am beginning to doubt it already.
Seems we are all just types, and there are few
indviduals left. In any case, let me see what you
have, will you. (She walks to counter where Clerk
and Bert show her various store items)
(Door opens. Chimes. Enter St. Pierre who goes
straight to other counter and speaks to Bess)

ST. PIERRE: How nice it is to live incognito. Be somebody
else, wear somebody else's clothes, meet some
body else's friends. For me, this—this is freedom,
this is liberty. I am taking a vacation from my own
identify. I can stand at the corner for hours now,
and everybody walks by, and nobody knows who
I really am, least of all the cops—this is a new
life for me. This is true freedom—

BESS: Just watch out that the real St. Pierre does not get
well. Besides—we have a customer, so—

ST. PIERRE: (Cringes and makes for the counter as if to hide
behind it. Then sees Cust 2, speaks to her) Oh yes,
we do, indeed. Pardon me, madame, pardon me,

but—may I, please? (Steps to her side) Would
you let me recommend this stone and this, and
one more, perhaps. (Produces stones, one after the
other, from his pockets) Oh how long, how long—
quousque tandem—have I been waiting to show
these stones to somebody worthy of them—

CUST 2: Well. I am glad you think I am—as you put it
—worthy—

ST. PIERRE: Oh no, madame, don't misunderstand me,
please—it's not you—I mean, it's the stones that
are worthy of you. These stones, madame,
(Grandly) I found them, discovered them myself,
in the jungles of Brazil, in a riverbed. Then I put
them in my pocket where they have remained
since and where time has polished them on long
journeys across land and sea, on horseback, on ski.
(Holds two stones up for Cust 2 to see)

CUST 2: They do look nice—unique, clean. You said you
found them? (Looks at St. P) It seems to me you
might have found them, but in a special way.

ST. PIERRE: Oh, madame, you are too much of a lady to
judge a man by his clothes or face. True, my suit is
old and tattered, and yours is rich and fine. But
behind them, inside of us, you are me and any
body, there is the soul, your soul, my soul, and our
hat, madame, is always unique, always special—

CUST 2: I have the feeling the price of these stones is going
up with every word. Well, what do you want for

them? You have sold me on them. I'll buy them—

ST. PIERRE: (More grandly) Sell? These stones? Impossible, madame. Never in your life, madame. How could I? Sell these stones for mere money? How could I? The only person who knows where they belong, where they have spent their early life. How could I? Sell—for money—never. But I tell you, madame. I shall take them back, back with you and for you. Back to Brazil where they came from. Yes, we shall take them back home to South America, restore to nature what is hers, be ecologists and do our good deed in the process. Well, madame, what do you say?

CUST 2: Well, I'll be damned. Are you suggesting...?

ST. PIERRE: Oh no, madame, I would not dare to suggest. On the other hand, I am. Yes. You must do it. We must do it. It is in our nature to be unique in being and action—you and I. Yes, I am suggesting, and I also suggest you don't think so much. Don't hesitate, I see it in your eyes. It spoils your gusto, your élan. You really want to do it. Yes, you do. (He puts his arm under hers and half pushes half drags her through the main door. Turns briefly) Good-bye, everybody. See you soon.

BESS: (Screams) Stop him! He has the stones, our stones. Stop him! (She rushes after the two but is intercepted by Lili who is entering through the main door)

LILI: Stop whom?

BESS: St. Pierre, Jack—he is gone, he's gone off with yet
        another woman. Stop him, somebody.

LILI: (Very quiet) St. Pierre—Jack—my—my father?
        No, it cannot be. It cannot be —

BESS: That's what I said, too.

BERT: Oh—let him go. Found himself another woman.
        Just what he likes: girlfriend, mother, money. Nice
        combination. Let him go. He'll be back in a year or
        two. He'll be back. Who needs him now, anyhow?

LILI: No, no. It cannot be. He cannot just go. I need him,
        I need him. Wait for me, please wait for me.
        (Rushes to front door where Bert catches her and
        holds her for a second. She wrenches free and runs
        through side door)

BESS: Nice scene. Enjoyed it, Bert?

BERT: I was only trying to stop her.

BESS: I saw what you did.

CLERK: And so did I.

BERT: (Angry) Stop your nagging, both of you, and
        your insinuations.

BESS: No offense intended, dear.

BERT: Stop it, I said. Help me unpack these shells, then
        go downstairs and wash them. More customers
        might be coming, any time. (Front door opens.
        Chimes. Enter Eric and Lawyer, both swaggering,
        arm in arm)

LAWYER: New life rises from old ruins. Let's drink some

more. To the new life.

CLERK: Steady now, both of you. Come over here and sit down. (Leads the two to sofa)

BESS: (Solicitously) Yes, come and sit down before you fall and get hurt. Here—how's that?

ERIC: (Leaning back in sofa) Fine, just fine. I went to his office this morning to see if he had any part-time work, as he promised me. Yes, he said, my part-time work was playing the guitar for him—Said he was so overworked—

LAWYER: So he played for me, and then we went to a bar— but how's business, anyway?

CLERK: Picking up, picking up.

LAWYER: Ha-ha—picking—picking up—isn't that what you called your playing, Eric? Fingerpicking. You must tell me more about this, and show me more. And we'll drink more to the new fingerpicking life. (Pulls pint bottle from coat) Here's to you all. Cheers. (Front door opens. Chimes. Enter Lili, dressed in same clothes as during first appearance)

LILI: They got away. I just couldn't keep up. But at least, I know where I am going.

BERT: Where, Lili?

LILI: Home.

CLERK: Home? You? I have a better idea. Let's all go to my home. Anybody interested?

BERT: I'll go with you, for a little while. The walk will do us good. The walk, the talk—Coming, Lili?

LILI: I guess so. What else is there? We must keep
moving, all of us.

LAWYER: Cheers for the new life. Keep moving and be a
part-timer. That's the secret: be yourself, part-
time. The hell with 8 to 6 routines, white and
blue collars.

ERIC: Hear, hear. In vino veritas—there's truth in your
bottle, sir.

LAWYER: Truth? What is truth? And who needs it?

BERT: Come on, you two, let's go. This is getting too
deep. It's beginning to make me ill. (Bert takes
arms of both women and steers them to exit by
front door. Bess spreads both arms and blocks
their way. Bert avoids confrontation by taking
Clerk and Lili out by side door. Bess shakes her
head, folds arms, waits for second)

BESS: Gone? They too? But they too will be back, won't
they? But meanwhile—what is left to me? What
is left to me? The Stone Box? Stone's General
Store? Yes, sir? At your service, sir? Service to
whom? Two drunk men? And whom I should
serve first? The old—well-heeled, well-oiled? Or
the young, the part-time cook-singer? Who shall
get them back to life, to work. I guess, service is
where you find it. What did Bert always say? 'My
freedom—is service.' Funny, I never
understood him, either. And now he's gone. Like

his brother—gone. And that leaves me—alone.
Mother Stone was right, after all. This is a world
where one can serve—where one must serve.
And so it shall be. (Steps resolutely toward sofa,
turns back to Lawyer and Eric) So it shall be.

ERIC AND LAWYER: (Struggling to get up) With cheers to the
new life. Cheers—cheers. (They try to drag Bess
down to sofa, but she shakes both off. They sit
down while she remains standing, arms folded,
looking first at audience and then after turning at
two men and store as curtain slowly falls)